MW00607728

THE PERFECT SCORECARD:

GETTING AN 'A' IN CYBERSECURITY
FROM YOUR BOARD OF DIRECTORS

Copyright 2021 SecurityScorecard

All rights reserved. No part of this publication may be reproduced, distributed, or transmitted in any form or by any means, including photocopying, recording, or other electronic or mechanical methods, without the prior written permission of the publisher, except in the case of brief quotations embodied in critical review and certain other noncommercial uses permitted by copyright law. For permission request, write to the publisher, addressed "Attention: Permissions Coordinator," at the address below.

ISBN: 978-0-578-93044-2

Front cover image by Natalia Talkowska

Illustrations by Natalia Talkowska

Printed by SecurityScorecard in the United States of America

First printing edition 2021

SecurityScorecard
111 West 33rd Street. FLR 11
New York, NY 10001

www.securityscorecard.com

The information provided in this book is for general informational and educational purposes only. The views expressed in this book are those of the individual authors in their individual capacities, not those of their respective employers, the other authors, or the publisher. Any advice or recommendations are made without guarantee on the part of the authors or publisher. The authors and publisher make no representations or warranties, express or implied, about (a) the completeness, accuracy, reliability, suitability, effectiveness, or applicability with respect to the information (including, without limitation, advice, strategies, and considerations) for any purpose and (b) any success you may have or achieve using the information. You accept the risk that results will differ for each individual and company. The information contained in this book is provided on an "as is" basis, including no representations or warranties that the content is correct and error-free. Any use of this information is at your own risk. All liability related to the content of this book, including with respect to actions taken or not taken based thereon, are hereby expressly disclaimed. For the purpose of this disclaimer, "author" includes those who wrote the content and those who are identified in the book who contributed to the content.

THE PERFECT SCORECARD:

GETTING AN 'A' IN CYBERSECURITY
FROM YOUR BOARD OF DIRECTORS

Aleksandr Yampolskiy, Ph.D.
CEO and Founder, SecurityScorecard

*This book is dedicated to my wife, Kira Yampolskiy,
and to my children, Ben and Maya.*

Acknowledgments

More than a decade ago, I was hired as the CISO at a rapidly growing e-commerce startup in New York. It was my first C-suite job and I moved fast, quickly recruiting a team and building a strategic plan in order to make an impact.

Three months into my tenure, I received an email from the chairman of our Board of Directors which said "Alex, I'd like to get an update on your security strategy."

I prepared an elaborate deck and rehearsed it a few times before going into the chairman's office. As I entered the glass-enclosed office with stacks of books organized neatly throughout, the chairman poured himself a cup of tea, flipped through my deck and said unflinchingly, "I don't think you are doing a good job."

It was a statement, not a question.

I was upset -- and surprised. "How could he think that, despite all the progress I outlined in front of him?" I thought. But I had no quantifiable way of proving that I was doing a good job.

The chairman paused, flipped through the deck some more and continued: "I don't think you are doing a good job, because I don't hear enough people complaining about you. If you were making enough changes, then more people would complain."

I brought on several key team members to ensure I was making integral changes to spur those complaints -- including Sam Kassoumeh, someone I grew to trust and rely on in the hardest of times. Several years after that initial conversation with the chairman, Sam and I came up with a dream of "computing a scorecard" for every company in the world. During our time working together, Sam and I often wondered if there was a viable way to have a quantifiable set of KPIs that are objective and non-intrusive to measure any company in the world and their security progress. We hadn't seen anything remotely like that in the market and so, we set out to create it -- and with it, SecurityScorecard was born.

During our discovery and iteration process, we discovered that CISOs are from Mars and board members are from Venus. The board understands the language of P&L, numbers, forecasts, yet rarely asks pointed questions about cyber hygiene. At the times when they ask, they don't know how to assess the quality of responses, and if their CISO knows what to do and how to do it.

Conversely, we found that CISOs are frustrated, because they are not getting the support and resources needed from the CEO and board to respond to the security issues they see. Most CISOs contend with large budget cuts, delayed security patches and more. Nowadays, the job of a CISO seems impossible as the world becomes more interconnected and attacks rise and increase in sophistication.

In this book, we assembled the best and most innovative thinkers in security and asked their advice for how security executives can best communicate to the board and alternately, what board members need to know to assess their security executives. The authors include top CISOs, advisors, generals, CEOs, Board members, practitioners - and I am grateful to each of them for the gems of wisdom they have shared with us in these pages.

I'd like to wholeheartedly thank all the co-authors in the book who shared their experiences candidly and transparently to benefit the community and to make the world safer:

- Mark Weatherford, Chief Strategy Officer at the National Cybersecurity Center
- Laura Deaner, Chief Information Security Officer at Northwestern Mutual
- Brian Stafford, Chief Executive Officer at Diligent Corporation
- Roota Almeida, Chief Information Security Officer at Delta Dental of NJ and CT
- Jonathan Dambrot & Rik Parker, Principals at KPMG Cybersecurity
- Derek Vadala, CEO, VisibleRisk
- Anthony Dagostino, Executive VP - Global Cyber and Technology Practice Leader at Lockton Companies
- Ray Mabus, Former Secretary of the United States Navy and current CEO of Mabus Group
- Brian Cincera, SVP & Chief Information Security Officer at Pfizer, Inc

- Moriah Hara, Head of Cybersecurity & Technology Risk, BMO Financial Group
- Adam Bishop, Director, Information Security at EPAM Systems
- Edna Conway, VP, Chief Security & Risk Officer at Azure, a Microsoft Corporation
- Charles Blauner, Partner & CISO in residence at Team8 and President of Cyber Aegis
- Dr. Taher Elgamal, Chief Technology Officer for Security at Salesforce

I would also like to thank my hardworking, innovative and inspirational colleagues at SecurityScorecard for what they do every day. My colleagues have helped me learn and practice better communication -- both as a CISO myself and now a CEO.

One person I'd like to single out is my business partner, Sam Kassoumeh. He helped me scale SecurityScorecard from two people to over 300 today, along with thousands of customers and partners. Sam, you are an inspirational leader, partner, executive, CISO, and most importantly, friend. I also want to call out SecurityScorecard's Chief of Staff Dolly Krishnaswamy, who we call the 'glue' that holds our company together. Dolly, thank you for helping me stay organized, efficient and always holding the bar higher and holding us to your standards.

Finally, on the family side: I'd like to thank my parents, Irina Lagutina and Vladimir Yampolskiy. They immigrated to the U.S. in search of better dreams and sacrificed a lot so that their children could have a better future.

Last but not least, this book is dedicated to my children, Ben and Maya, and my amazing wife Kira. Each of them has shaped me into a better human being and helped me achieve the impossible by serving as a patient advisor, board member and counsel throughout my career.

I welcome any comments, feedback and general communications about the book. Please feel free to contact me at PerfectScoreBook@securityscorecard.io or via LinkedIn.

Contents

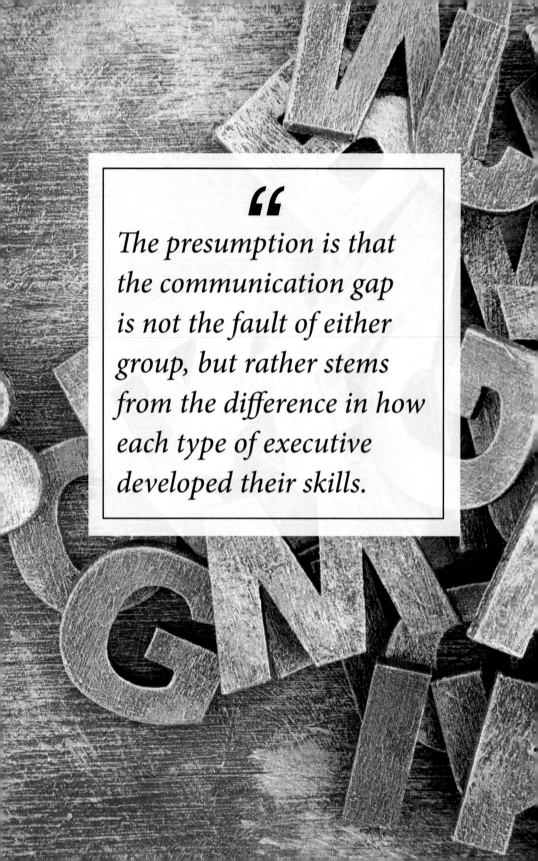

> **"**
> *The presumption is that the communication gap is not the fault of either group, but rather stems from the difference in how each type of executive developed their skills.*

Introduction

Improving Communications Between CISOs and Senior Executives

**DR. EDWARD AMOROSO, CEO, TAG CYBER
AND ALEX YAMPOLSKIY, CEO AND CO-FOUNDER,
SECURITYSCORECARD**

A challenge exists in modern organizations: to improve the quality and effectiveness of formal and informal communications between the Chief Information Security Officer (CISO) and other senior executives, including the C-suite and board members. This publication presents action plans to help CISOs and senior executives find common ground.

Introduction: Understanding the challenge

We've all witnessed the struggles that technology experts often have when trying to communicate with less technical colleagues. The image comes to mind of the IT help desk expert attempting in vain to explain to a confused employee how a task might be accomplished. The reverse is also common, where an employee tries to make a request from technical staff, but struggles to explain what they are actually trying to accomplish.

A similar communication challenge exists between senior executive staff and enterprise security leadership teams. Generally, business executives and CISOs have different backgrounds, and as a result, often speak in much different languages. The result is that communication between CISOs and senior executives is often lacking–hence, the need for this discussion.

Below we offer some practical tips for both groups in the form of recommended action plans. The presumption is that the communication gap is not the fault of either group, but rather stems from the differences in how each type of executive developed their skills. By focusing on proposed action plans for both CISOs and senior executives, an organization nurtures the possibility that this information-sharing gap might be minimized, and this will reduce risk.

Action plan for CISOs

The action plan recommended for CISOs is focused primarily on curating their communication skills, but perhaps not in the manner one might expect. Most advice for CISOs to date has been to simplify their explanations of cybersecurity, presumably because senior executives are ill-equipped to understand complex technical issues. While aspects of this view might be true, our advice to CISOs actually follows a somewhat different path.

Instead of "dumbing down" complex technical and compliance issues related to cybersecurity for senior executives, CISOs are encouraged to improve the quality of their presentations. Discussions held with senior executives should be clear and correct, but they do not require hand holding as if they are Luddites. Instead, communications should be improved and sharpened. Senior executives are intelligent, and they can keep up.

Most senior executives recognize the risk an immature cybersecurity program poses to their company. Recognizing and quantifying, however, are two different things. For example, a decade ago, building a robust security infrastructure and program involved creating a fortress around on-premises data centers. CISOs felt more in control because data was contained within their own environments. The rise of digital transformation and cloud-based resources changed the CISO's security model. Today, an organizations' security posture relies on their technology partners' security postures.

The specific action plan recommended for CISOs to improve their communications with senior executives includes three points, each of which can be initiated immediately. All three can be curated by the CISO, with emphasis on continual improvement.

Action #1: Never underplay the real challenges of cybersecurity to executives.

More than ever before, technology drives collaborative business processes. The rise of turnkey cloud technologies creates a hyper-connected ecosystem, shifting the IT model from data fortress to data ecosystem. Additionally, to enable their workforces, companies give various levels of access to a number of clients, suppliers, and consultants.

Every new access point—whether human or technology—increases the challenges that CISOs face, and they need to give their senior leadership team a realistic picture of these new risks. They also need to find metrics and key performance indicators that make sense in this new hyper-connected ecosystem. Explaining these challenges can be difficult, but it is not impossible.

Each connected location is a domino in the middle of that IT infrastructure. If one domino falls, the ones around it become less stable and can topple. The hyper-connected ecosystem works the same way, which is why security ratings provide valuable insight for senior leadership teams and boards of directors. Organizations can use security ratings to track their safest and riskiest business partners as a way to gain insight into the stability of each partner "domino" throughout the supply chain.

As a member of the C-suite, a CISO must bring business acumen along with security expertise to bridge the divide between security functions and the C-suite. CISOs can accomplish this by providing their leadership and directors with visibility into ecosystem complexity using business language, such as risk and financials, to get everyone on the same page. Giving the team an understanding of risk in a way that aligns with their objectives is a way to move toward a more robust cybersecurity posture.

Action #2: Ensure that cybersecurity reports provide the right information for the audience.

CISOs, senior executives, and directors all understand the importance of cybersecurity. CISOs need to remove technical jargon from their reporting and provide security reports that offer value. Security reporting should be simple, objective, and actionable. A simple board report is one that provides easy-to-understand prescriptive and measurable remediation activities. For example, a CISO might want to create metrics that align with a cybersecurity framework, such as NIST, and use the high-level categories of Identify, Protect, Detect, Respond, and Recover. The report does not need to get into the technical details but provide data that enables informed decision making. The focus should be on understanding current maturity as compared to target maturity, using technical details as illustrative examples.

Reports must provide objective, independently verifiable analyses. Even in its most simple form, a board report needs to align security maturity with technical weaknesses. An audience-aware report uses the metrics as the supporting documentation for the business-level highlight. If leadership or directors want to drill down into how the CISO determined the maturity level, the evidence should enable independent analysis.

The most difficult part of creating a business-audience report is making it extensible across the complex, hyper-connected ecosystem. Gaining visibility into third- and fourth-party risks is the primary challenge organizations and CISOs face in a digitally transformed world. Security ratings provide the visibility that organizations need by going beyond traditional point-in-time reports. With continuous monitoring that takes an outside-in approach, security ratings offer at-a-glance visibility into a given vendor's or vendor ecosystem's risk.

When CISOs take an audience-centric approach to discussing security risk, they build stronger internal stakeholder relationships and enable better security outcomes.

Action #3: Become a true business partner to drive value.

In order to become a true business partner, the job of the CISO is not to say no but to help their peers come up with secure solutions to business problems. The CISO who approaches their relationships from a value-generation perspective for their company's customers will succeed.

For example, when I, Alex, was CISO at Gilt Groupe, I was concerned with not only securing the company's digital assets, but also with delivering value to the customers shopping on our public site. We integrated a service which would notify users if their passwords and accounts were compromised so they could change their passwords immediately. We drove value for the company by putting a secure NortonLifeLock badge on our checkout site, which improved our purchase conversion rate. At every turn, I aimed to not only be a support function, but to help the business from a profits and loss perspective.

As a Team Lead for Security Engineering at Goldman Sachs, I took a similar approach. When the opportunity arose to launch a Chinese internet trading service, I jumped at the chance to generate millions in new revenue while applying my security expertise.

Cybersecurity is now a business-critical initiative, and it's up to boards and members of the C-suite to work together to drive value for their organizations.

Action plan for senior executives

Just as CISOs must be attentive to their communication approach with the senior executives in the organization, the reverse obligation is also true. This prompts the recommended action plan listed below for C-suite executives and board members. The objective is to improve the quality of all formal and informal discussions, information sharing sessions, feedback processes, and other forms of interaction with the enterprise security team—which includes the CISO.

Just as with our advice for CISOs, the specific action plan recommended for executives includes three points–each of which can also be initiated immediately. Unlike CISOs, however, who come to the communication with the expectation that they will need to make adjustments, it might be more difficult for experienced executives to adjust their approach. If this becomes too big of a hurdle, some self-introspection is recommended.

Action #1: Take the time to self educate on cybersecurity using all available resources.

Just as CISOs must meet executive leadership where they are in their cybersecurity journey, leadership has a responsibility to gain a better understanding of technology. At a high level, leadership needs to understand the basic elements of digital transformation so they can make informed decisions around choosing technologies.

For example, this might mean understanding, on a basic level, that a device is an access point that malicious actors can exploit. It also means understanding why—not necessarily how—applying security patch updates to software and firmware mitigates risk.

Just as senior executives and directors have learned to extract the important findings in financial reports, they need to be able to extract fundamental data from security reports.

Action #2: Embrace cyber resilience.

While it might be tempting to require that a CISO promise complete security, the hyper-connected ecosystems necessary for maintaining modern business operations make that an impossible dream. Just as CISOs need to set up their senior leadership and boards for success, the same must be done in return.

CISOs need a leadership team that understands data breaches are inevitable. Rather than looking to drive risk to zero, senior leadership teams should make sure that CISOs focus on cyber resilience. This means giving them the tools necessary for improving detection and recovery times. Senior executives and directors should ensure they fund initiatives that reduce recovery time, enhance communications, and provide clarity over proper recovery steps.

Action #3: Encourage CISOs to share complexity if such detail is relevant.

Modern CISOs need to be business-aware, but their value to the company is their technical knowledge. As much as they need to step away from technical jargon, they still need to meaningfully explain technical issues.

Technical issues have a large impact on the choices companies make. For example, most organizations use cloud-based applications. Each connection point, or API, is a potential risk. If a CISO suggests that the company not deploy an application, the senior leadership team needs to ask why.

Senior executives and directors must question their CISOs purposefully, and they can do that by understanding the reasoning behind their suggestions. Senior executives need to work with their CISOs to understand risk, not to simply defer on all technology decisions.

Finding common ground

The ultimate goal for improving communications between CISOs and senior executives is to reduce enterprise cyber risk—and this should be the primary focus. To properly identify, assess, measure, and optimize decisions regarding cybersecurity threats, the CISO and executive team must be on the same page. Several other benefits, however, do result from this improved communication, including the following:

- Expanded employee career options: When the CISO communicates more effectively with the senior executive team, the result can be a more intimate alliance between the security team and rest of the company. This has the effect of opening and expanding career options for security team members in other parts of the organization—and the reverse is also true.

- Improved diversity in decision making: Improved communication between the CISO and senior executive team improves the diversity in decision making for the organization. Security-related matters have often been left out of major decisions, such as mergers with insecure companies and outsourcing to insecure suppliers. These problems can be avoided by improving diversity of input.

- Accelerated enablement of digital transformation: The ultimate goal of digital transformation requires avoidance of bad outcomes from hackers and enablement of safe operation for bold new means of automation. Including the CISO in this high-level discussion will improve the odds that the digital transformation initiatives will avoid any negative security consequences.

Successful organizations are built on a foundation of trust and respect. Most companies adopt technologies that enhance collaboration which ultimately reinforces these fundamental characteristics.

Dr. Ed Amoroso is founder and current Chief Executive Officer of TAG Cyber LLC, a global cyber security advisory, training, consulting, and media services company supporting hundreds of companies across the world. Ed recently retired from AT&T after thirty-one years of service, beginning in Unix security R&D at Bell Labs and culminating as Senior Vice President and Chief Security Officer of AT&T from 2004 to 2016. Ed has been Adjunct Professor of Computer Science at the Stevens Institute of Technology for the past twenty-seven years, where he has introduced nearly two thousand graduate students to the topic of information security. He is also affiliated with the Tandon School of Engineering at NYU as a research professor, and the Applied Physics Laboratory at Johns Hopkins University as a senior advisor. He is author of six books on cybersecurity and dozens of major research and technical papers and articles in peer-reviewed and major publications.

Aleksandr Yampolskiy is a globally recognized cybersecurity innovator, leader, and expert. As co-founder and chief executive officer, Alex has led the company since its beginnings in 2013 to become one of the world's most trusted cybersecurity brands. His vision is to create a new language for cybersecurity by enabling people to work collaboratively across the enterprise and with external parties to build a more secure ecosystem. Prior to founding the company, Alex was a hands-on CTO at Cinchcast and BlogTalkRadio, the largest online talk radio and podcast hosting platform. Prior to that, he led security and compliance at Gilt Groupe, where he managed all aspects of IT infrastructure security, secure application development, and PCI compliance. Alex has a B.A. in mathematics and computer science from New York University and a Ph.D. in Cryptography from Yale University.

> **"**
> *Creativity is a force multiplier that allows the CISO to be more responsive and nourish better team performance.*

1

Do We Have the Right Cybersecurity Leader?

MARK WEATHERFORD, CHIEF STRATEGY OFFICER AND BOARD MEMBER, NATIONAL CYBERSECURITY CENTER

A few years ago, a CISO colleague invited me to give a cybersecurity threat briefing to his company's board of directors at their regularly-scheduled quarterly board meeting. After giving my threat presentation and fielding a few questions, my colleague gave his regular quarterly report to the board. The chairman of the board asked a couple of business risk- and revenue-focused questions and was clearly not getting the kind of self-assured responses he expected. The chairman kept asking questions, and it quickly became obvious that my colleague was out of his depth and couldn't speak intelligently on any topic beyond cybersecurity. The chairman finally ended what had become an awkward inquisition by saying, "You don't really understand how this company makes money, do you?"

It was one of the most professionally uncomfortable meetings I've ever sat through in my life, and I'm sure everyone else in the room felt the same.

The colleague I mentioned above is a good example of how security leaders are often promoted into executive roles without the requisite business experience to truly deserve a seat at the table. Far too many CISOs come directly from a technical or operational role, without the appropriate conditioning or experience to interact with the vast business diversity of most boards. These folks are used to rolling up their sleeves and getting their hands dirty when it comes to cybersecurity but are often not yet ready for the boardroom. Quite simply, while they understand cybersecurity risk, they have never contemplated economic risk, competitive risk, or even regulatory risk outside of the security realm.

Looking beyond the resume

Many CISOs look like fantastic cybersecurity leaders on paper. However, when you get beyond their resume and credentials, you find holes or gaps in their leadership or management experience that can seriously impact their ability to function in an executive role. So how can you tell if your organization has the right cybersecurity leader?

Just like any executive or senior leader role, there is a wide range of qualities you should be seeking in a CISO—confidence, experience, creativity, vision, and integrity. It's hard to imagine anyone with vast responsibility in any company who doesn't exude these characteristics.

Confidence

I believe that the most important board expectation of a CISO is confidence. Since cybersecurity is an acknowledged esoteric skill for most board directors, they must have confidence that the CISO implicitly understands their role. Perhaps more importantly though, the CISO must be able to demonstrate with conviction that they have the

skill to keep the company headed in the right direction without undue cyber-drama that derails the company's strategic plans.

Confidence does not mean smugness or arrogance, and board members should be wary of a CISO with the holier-than-thou attitude that is unfortunately far too common in the technology arena. A good cybersecurity leader should be confident enough in their knowledge and their communication skills to focus on what the board needs to know, and further, to anticipate what may be arcane to non-technologists.

If a CISO can't inspire the confidence of the board, it becomes incredibly difficult to influence the organization to accept security as a core component of its culture and mission. To be successful in their role, the CISO must have influence within the C-suite, the board, and the rest of the company. Because security is realistically a part of everyone's job, the CISO must be able to influence everyone in the organization. This requires implicit confidence.

Experience

It goes without saying, but experience is critical for a CISO. And not just the indispensable technical cybersecurity experience. A CISO should have a wide variety of leadership experience, including finance and budgeting, strategy, legal, and regulatory. Just like any other executive, the modern CISO needs to be a well-rounded student of the business, and not just the 'geek in a black t-shirt.'

This doesn't, however, mean that a first-time CISO can't be a good CISO. A new CISO who has diligently prepared to be a member of the C-suite should have accumulated many of the experiences necessary for success. They may not have a decade's worth of hard knocks, but the security professional who has been proactive and focused on seeking the requisite experience is typically the kind of person other leaders recognize and want to see succeed.

Creativity

A great CISO also needs to be creative, because no security organization has all the resources—people, funding, or tools—they feel they need to succeed. Creativity is a force multiplier that allows the CISO to be more responsive, nourish better team performance, and influence higher levels of overall security than might be reasonably expected within resource boundaries. Creativity is a moderately intangible quality but can be sufficiently appraised through focused discussion and inquiry.

It's a two-way street

Boards and CISOs often misunderstand each other. Boards have a broad and diverse set of responsibilities, most of which the CISO has never been exposed to. This is a blind spot for many CISOs and they are often so focused on their cybersecurity responsibilities that they forget they are simply a supporting component of the overall business. Boards, on the other hand, need to acknowledge that cybersecurity is not just a feature but a business imperative, and they need to become more well-versed in the cyber threat and vulnerability world that CISOs live in.

It's critical that the board and the CISO understand each other, and each should be prepared to spend time educating, and when necessary, coaching the other. The CISO must be as comfortable in a business conversation as they are in a cybersecurity discussion, and understanding how cyber risks impact overall revenue is critical. CISOs must be able to communicate that cyber is simply another risk in the overall portfolio of risks their company faces. Like the CISO mentioned at the beginning of this chapter, all must be students of the business and understand how their organization generates revenue.

While that CISO was certainly negligent for not understanding the business, the executive team as well as the board bear some responsibility for assuming basic comprehension. Boards often pigeonhole CISOs as technology geeks, and while boards are not often directly involved in the CISO hiring process, they should have more than a once-a-quarter familiarity.

Communication between a CISO and the board is important, and the earlier it begins, the better.

As security incidents develop and threats occur, a board needs to know and trust that the CISO can manage issues professionally. Being proactive about that relationship, reaching out and getting to know the CISO, is the first step to knowing whether you have the right cybersecurity leader.

Mark Weatherford is the Chief Strategy Officer and on the Board of Directors at the National Cybersecurity Center. He is the Founding Partner at Aspen Chartered where he provides cybersecurity consulting and advisory services to public and private sector organizations around the world. Mark has held a variety of executive level cybersecurity roles including Global Information Security Strategist at Booking Holdings, Chief Cybersecurity Strategist at vArmour, a Principal at The Chertoff Group, Chief Security Officer at the North American Electric Reliability Corporation, and Chief Information Security Officer for the state of Colorado. In 2008, he was appointed by Governor Arnold Schwarzenegger to serve as California's first Chief Information Security Officer, and in 2011 he was appointed by the Obama Administration as Deputy Under Secretary for Cybersecurity at the U.S. Department of Homeland Security. Mark is a former naval officer where he served as a cryptologist and was Director of Navy Computer Network Defense Operations, Director of the Navy Computer Incident Response Team (NAVCIRT), and established the Navy's first operational red team. He is an investor and on the Advisory Board of several cybersecurity technology companies where he has a very successful track record in helping multiple startups move to an acquisition.

> **"**
> *In a digitally transformed world, a CISO must marry the organization's business and technology goals.*

2

How to Test Your CISO

**LAURA DEANER, CISO
NORTHWESTERN MUTUAL**

Over the last twenty years, cybersecurity professionals and boards of directors have witnessed an overwhelming digital revolution. The sheer interconnectedness of the world changes the role CISOs play in an organization's success. From a cybersecurity perspective, cloud technologies change how CISOs need to manage data security, yet traditional security principles fail to address these new risks adequately. Cybercriminals take advantage of these vulnerabilities, which makes being a CISO more challenging than ever. As directors look to build resilient security teams, they need to find leaders who meet their business and technology needs. With that in mind, here are questions boards should ask their CISOs so they can create meaningful business and security relationships.

How do you view your relationship with us?

Every board member is ultimately accountable for understanding their organization's risk. To fulfill their obligations, directors need a CISO who believes in transparency and full disclosure. Boards need to know their actual risk profile, not just the rosy picture that the CISO thinks they want to hear. By asking how candidates view their relationship with the board, directors can gain valuable insight into how this relationship can protect their organization's interests.

How do you feel technology enables a company's objectives?

In a digitally transformed world, a CISO must marry the organization's business and technology goals. As organizations adopt more cloud resources, they need a CISO who understands these technologies' fundamentals, such as the inner workings of TCP/IP handshake or the OSI model. Without a basic technology background, CISOs cannot communicate with their teams effectively. CISOs need to ask their teams the right questions, then translate those answers back to their boards. Fundamentally, they act as a board's technology interpreter, presenting the relevant risk information that enables directors' success.

What is your philosophy on measuring risk?

Beyond technical capabilities, CISOs need to prove that their approach to risk aligns with the board's strategy. For example, CISOs with technology backgrounds may be able to talk about headline-making data events for days, but they also need to explain the risks that those incidents pose to their own company. A CISO may measure risk based on risk appetite statements, risk thresholds in those statements, or risk taxonomy methodologies. The right CISO will have a philosophy that aligns with the board's, ensuring a standard approach to both technology and business risk.

How do you believe cybersecurity fits into the organization's business objectives?

As part of their technology interpreter role, CISOs need to understand their organization's business goals to translate information security risk into business risk. The board and CISO need to share a vision for how technology and business objectives overlap. Boards need to ensure that their CISOs understand business goals. For example, organizations with multiple business lines or companies under one umbrella may have individual risk appetites for each. The CISO needs to understand the interconnection and individuality across the company's portfolio, using both security and business acumen to create a complete picture of its overarching risk.

How do you measure impact?

As technology subject matter experts, CISOs have a unique

relationship with their boards. While directors know how to read CFO- or CEO-supplied financial reports, they often rely heavily on their CISOs to explain how cybersecurity risks and incidents impact their organizations. This dynamic requires a relationship built on transparency with metrics as the foundation. CISOs should provide a description of metrics and offer dashboards that give their directors visibility into the organization's overall security profile. By measuring everything, directors gain the transparency needed to build long-term trusting relationships with their CISOs.

How do you plan to solve the most significant threats facing the organization?

This question provides visibility into a potential CISO's personality. CISOs with a full range of business and technology acumen solve only one part of the security puzzle. Humility, an often-overlooked trait in cybersecurity, matters just as much. In a world where the occurrence of security incidents is a matter of when not if, CISOs who believe they can stop everything should be a red flag for directors. A better response focuses on managing cyber risk as effectively as possible while recognizing that situations will occur. A strong CISO will focus on resilience rather than elimination.

What does the principle of agility mean to you?

Enterprise-wide agility requires iteration based on learning from previous incidents. Thus, boards need to understand that rapidly pivoting is not the key to cyber resilience or at-scale agility. Boards should look for CISOs who focus on incorporating learnings into the process and approaching agility from a team perspective.

How do you approach collaborating with and influencing others?

Board members understand the internal politics of their organization and need CISOs who can manage those relationships. Information security is a team initiative, meaning effective CISOs understand that having a single edict from above fails. Regardless of a CISO's reporting structure, the person chosen needs to work with and answer to various internal stakeholders. A strong CISO gains buy-in by effectively convincing these stakeholders that security matters to them and their objectives.

How do you approach compliance in the context of security?

While compliance is not equal to security, CISOs need to understand how they fit into an organization's legal and regulatory risk programs. Every organization takes a different approach to compliance. In some cases, a CISO needs to collaborate with a Chief Privacy Officer. In other cases, the partners might be General Counsel and Chief Risk Officer. The key to any organization's compliance program is ensuring that the CISO understands that privacy is an important, if not the most important, subset of security. A CISO's compliance approach should match the board's vision to ensure that the controls in place protect data and meet increasingly stringent compliance requirements.

What do we expect from a CISO?

Choosing the right CISO requires a complete understanding of the job's difficulty. Boards need to know that their CISOs can live up to expectations, but must also set realistic expectations. Security professionals never stop working because cybercriminals never stop trying to infiltrate systems, networks, and software. As much as CISOs need to be the right partner for their boards, directors need to be the right partner for their CISOs. Boards need to recognize that no individual, team, or department will be able to stop every single threat. They must readjust their perspectives on data protection and protect CISOs' mental and physical well-being. Only by working together and understanding one another can CISOs and boards establish robust cybersecurity programs that protect data, reputation, and financial stability.

Laura Deaner is the new Chief Information Security Officer at Northwestern Mutual where she leads the Enterprise Information Risk & Cybersecurity team and is responsible for spearheading Northwestern Mutual's Information Security strategy. Prior to her appointment at Northwestern Mutual, she was the first female CISO of S&P Global, responsible for establishing and driving the enterprise information security vision and program. She leverages her twenty-one years working in security for multi-national Fortune 500 companies to build effective and robust information security programs by aligning deep technical expertise with executive business vision and support. She was previously the first named CISO at PRNewswire where she built a comprehensive security practice from the ground up. Laura holds a Bachelor's degree in Computer Science from Old Dominion University in Virginia. She is a member of several information security and technology societies including OWASP, WiCyS, ISC2, and Society of Women Engineers (SWE). She's featured in Women Know Cyber – 100 Fascinating Females Fighting Cybercrime. Laura is an advocate for diversity and inclusion in technology as well as her field of Cyber Security. She serves as a council member of the S&P Global Diversity and Inclusion Council, which is tasked with fostering a diverse and inclusive environment. Her accomplishments as a council member have included revamping the Employee Resource Groups, adding sentiment and data driven metrics to enhance the community goals. She established partnerships with various organizations, such as Girls Who Code, to build diverse talent pipelines. Laura is a frequently requested speaker and respected thought leader, recognized for her innovative leadership and strong business acumen. She has participated in the World Economic Forum's Global Futures Council on Cybersecurity as a co-chair leading a group of subject matter experts in solving cyber challenges. She serves on the Board of Directors for the Financial Services Information Sharing and Analysis Center (FS-ISAC), an industry consortium dedicated to reducing cyber risk in the global financial system. FS-ISAC has 7000 plus financial institutions, 15,000 users in the 70 jurisdictions to ensure the mission is accomplished. As a board member, she continues to encourage more participation in sharing timing cyber information which is action oriented at a global scale.

> **"**
> *CISOs need practical strategies to improve their interactions with their boards of directors and C-suite executives to gain their confidence...*

3

CISOs and the Board

BRIAN STAFFORD, CEO
DILIGENT CORPORATION

Picture this: A Chief Information Security Officer enters a boardroom—or, these days, a virtual meeting—to have a conversation with a company's leadership about the risks and security issues their organization faces. The CISO does one of two things: they begin a detailed, technical presentation that is increasingly met with glazed-over looks from board members, or even worse, provide a cursory "all's well" report that arouses suspicion from the board. Either approach highlights a potential disconnect that, if not adequately addressed, puts companies at risk in an increasingly complex threat environment.

Diligent Corporation—a global governance company with 19,000 clients and more than 700,000 board members and senior executive users—has worked with enough CISOs over the years to recognize the struggles they have in connecting with the board members and leadership they are tasked with serving. Boards often dismiss a confusing or inarticulate presentation, leaving them vulnerable to serious risks or paralyzed by inaction.

With the right focus, presentation and preparation, CISOs and boards of directors can build strong and effective relationships that create trust ensure understanding, and support decision-making at the highest levels. CISOs need practical strategies to improve their interactions with their boards of directors and C-suite executives to gain their confidence, ensure their comfort, and protect the security of their company. Ultimately, many if not most CISOs will need to adjust their existing approach so that directors and executives have the right tools and information at the right moment. CISOs can begin by focusing on communication, offering perspective, promoting collaboration, and ensuring accountability.

Communication

Interactions between CISOs and boards need to begin with clear and effective communication. Essentially, CISOs need to make their information accessible to their audience by aligning the technical with the business objective, not by simplifying the presentation or removing important information. Having and demonstrating technical expertise provides little benefit if the listener cannot discern critical information needed for setting the direction of the organization.

To be successful, a CISO should be able to articulate security priorities in a way that connects with leadership by:

1. Stripping any technical jargon from their language and presentation.
2. Finding ways to express their main points without relying on industry terminology.

3. Quantifying information in terms that relate to the board's
    concerns, like overseeing risk and risk mitigation or investing in
    growth and value creation.

In today's governance environment, cyber risk is often the domain of
board audit committees, populated by CFOs and others with financial
analysis backgrounds, who focus primarily on the interplay of risk
and dollars. The successful, effective CISO presents cyber in terms of
numbers, resource allocation, and ROI benefit per dollar spent, creating
a baseline of trust and understanding that can help guide decisions
going forward.

Perspective

The board's responsibility involves choices and trade-offs based on
risk appetite, potential damage, and finite resource allocation. As a
result, their viewpoint covers all facets of an organization's operating
ability, which makes them an immensely useful resource. However, this
viewpoint also requires them to make decisions about how to distribute
their time, energy, and dollars. Board members need to know how risks
impact the financial bottom line because they have a fiduciary duty

to investors and shareholders. They need to address business issues such as capital and time investments, and need to know which risks are more likely to impact the company's financial stability or increase operational costs. To do their job, board members need the CISO to clearly prioritize risks like potential human error, system technology failure, external events, or internal processes failure.

Risk factors, of course, vary significantly depending on the nature of an organization and its circumstances. At Diligent, for example, client data is the most precious charge. As a result, the company remains highly focused on any risk that could lead to leaks, breaches, or incursions around client data. This priority means the security team remains closely engaged in protecting any processes, systems, or functions that might potentially come into contact with that information. Since Diligent's executive leadership and board of directors prioritize that risk, the company expends significant resources in service of that protection.

An effective CISO approaches board conversations with an eye toward how cybersecurity risks impact business priorities, offering clarity for board members who want to find the right path forward. A good CISO is never going to promise that they can ensure that all risks will be effectively eliminated by expending vast resources across risk areas. Similarly, a good CISO will never tell a company to save their dollars, ignore potential issues, and hope for the best. But an effective CISO can lay out the likelihood of various risks, potential impacts of those risks, and provide useful context for the board's decisions and deliberations. By understanding the board's perspective, a CISO helps the members make choices about the best way to allocate resources.

Collaboration

CISOs are a critical part of the senior management team when they understand how they fit into the overall organizational structure—and demonstrate that in their board interactions. Although it may sound counterintuitive, responsibility over data and risk mitigation does not necessarily mean the CISO is the risk owner. Because risk belongs to the business, the senior leadership team is responsible for managing and mitigating risk, ultimately providing the information that the board needs to engage in meaningful oversight as part of its fiduciary duty.

Most CISOs are working closely with other parts of the IT organization who are data custodians, managing data on behalf of the business who owns the data. While the data owner gives information technology professionals the task of protecting information, the board still needs guidance around how that protection impacts the organization's financials. The board then uses the information to focus its attention and resources. They own the risk, and they should have the information they need to make choices to mitigate that risk.

Collaboration also provides mutual benefit. In order to direct activities and priorities, CISOs need to be familiar with the board's risk acceptance statement. With this knowledge, the CISO can run the appropriate programs and risk treatment actions to meet the board's strategic needs. CISOs need board members to ask questions and engage in dialogue because they need to know the board's perspective.

This cyclical relationship requires CISOs to provide the board with the right questions to ask so the board can engage in the necessary due diligence to challenge the CISO's program execution. These questions can be as simple as:

- What are our top risks and what are the risk drivers?
- What is the company's inherent risk profile?
- What would we need to do in order to protect ourselves effectively against the risks we face?
- Are the risks we face generally increasing, or generally decreasing?
- Are we expending an appropriate amount of resources on our

cybersecurity protections?

- What level of security have we already achieved—and what prevents us from being more secure?

Ultimately, the relationship between a CISO and a governing board is symbiotic. Both need each other to work effectively, and a positive relationship benefits both parties and the entire organization.

Accountability

CISOs need the board to hold them accountable and vice versa. The board needs to hold the CISO accountable for data security plans while the CISO needs to hold the board accountable for understanding risk impact.

That's why CISOs should establish clear and consistent metrics tied to business outcomes to better articulate how security functions are performing and improving over time.

These metrics can include:

- The overall number of security incidents over a period of time and how that impacted the company's security posture
- The average time it took to detect security threats and how that ties to operational costs
- The average time it took to respond to an ongoing threat or attack and how that impacted the cost of the data security event
- The average time it took to make the vulnerable area secure again and how that impacted the cost of the data security event
- The way the organization's security compares with its peers and similar organizations, using a clear, concise number or reading, and how that impacts the organization's competitive advantage

Consistent measures of accountability tied to business outcomes build a stronger relationship between the CISO and the board.

Business-focused security metrics ease conversations with non-technical leadership while also giving the board a clear tool set for measuring CISO performance, creating subject matter familiarity, and bolstering trust. Accountability based on clear and consistent metrics enables a better-informed decision-making process around program implementation and execution.

The relationship between a board and a CISO is incredibly important at a time when technology is ubiquitous. As organizations use technology systems in new and unfamiliar ways, the threat surface has expanded beyond its usual capacity. To protect data and ensure continued organizational success, CISOs need to communicate effectively, put threats in perspective, foster collaboration, and drive accountability. By doing these four things, CISOs will help ensure a more effective organization—and a grateful board.

Brian Stafford is Chief Executive Officer of Diligent Corporation, the leading provider of modern governance software. Diligent's Modern Governance Platform is used globally by more than 700,000 Board members and senior executives including 50% of the Fortune 1000, 70% of the FTSE 100, and 65% of the ASX 100. Diligent's solutions span secure board and leadership collaboration, operational governance, and advanced governance analytics, empowering leading organizations achieve better outcomes for all stakeholders. Brian assumed the role of CEO in March 2015 with the mission of providing organizations with technology, insights and processes to turn governance into a competitive advantage. Diligent is backed by some of world's leading investors – Insight Partners, Blackstone Group and Clearlake Capital. Brian previously served as a Partner at McKinsey & Company, where he founded and led its Growth Stage Tech Practice. While there, he concentrated on helping Software-as-a-Service (SaaS) companies accelerate growth. Prior to his tenure at McKinsey, Brian was the Founder, President and CEO of an automotive spin off of Trilogy Software. Brian is the coauthor of Governance in the Digital Age. Brian holds a master's degree in Computer Science from the University of Chicago and a bachelor's degree in Science from the Wharton School at the University of Pennsylvania. Brian, his wife, and their two young children live in Baltimore, Maryland.

"

Whether an organization has experienced a ransomware attack or not, it needs to mitigate the vulnerabilities that often lead to them.

4

Ransomware: How to Deal With It, and What It Means to the Board

ROOTA ALMEIDA, CHIEF INFORMATION SECURITY OFFICER, DELTA DENTAL OF NEW JERSEY AND CONNECTICUT

Security professionals talk a lot about how cybercriminals continuously evolve their methodologies. Still, they often have a hard time providing examples of how malicious actors react to security teams' defensive activities. Historically, a ransomware attack would start with a social engineering attack that deposits a malicious ransomware executable program on a device. Once on the device, the software enables attackers to move within the organization's systems, networks, and software. Cybercriminals then encrypt data, making it useless, and only release it once the organization pays the requested ransom. To mitigate the risk these attacks pose to financial stability, organizations engaged in better backup processes, reducing the downtime a ransomware attack can cause and helping them avoid paying to have data released.

The game changer: Credential and data theft

Over the last year, security professionals have seen a change in how ransomware attacks work and an uptick in these incidents. Newer ransomware attacks not only encrypt the organization's data, they also steal sensitive information. While traditional ransomware attacks focused on obfuscating data, recent attacks focus on stealing credentials, often through phishing attacks. By leveraging stolen credentials, criminals can gain access to the organization's IT stack and steal data. This new approach renders backup protections useless. The company still has its information, but so does the attacker who is more than willing to expose it publicly.

These up-leveled ransomware attacks change the game for organizations. In the past, they could refuse to pay the ransom since data backups prevented business interruption. Now, they need to contend with the potential that the cybercriminals will expose the stolen data publicly, which leaves them facing the reputational risk associated with a typical data breach. Whether an organization has experienced a ransomware attack or not, it needs to mitigate the vulnerabilities that often lead to them.

Everyone Is a Target Because No One Is a Target

Even more troubling, cybercriminals rarely appear to be targeting specific organizations. They send out feelers and see what sticks, hoping to make a quick buck. For example, when the pandemic stay-at-home orders began, several cyberattacker groups refused to target hospitals, noting that those organizations were on the front lines. Despite these declarations, several hospitals found themselves subject

to cyberattacks. While news outlets reported an increase in attacks against the healthcare industry, attacks across industry verticals were also rising.

To receive payment time and again, cybercriminals must gain victim trust. If the victims do not trust cybercriminals to keep their promises, the organizations will choose not to pay the ransom. Working through negotiations with the "customer service" representatives, organizations and their negotiators can bring down the ransom value and get information returned to them. While this saves them in the present, it does not protect them for the future. This trust extends only to the immediate transaction, not future attack attempts.

Best practices: Cybersecurity awareness and segmentation

The rapid evolution of ransomware requires organizations to keep pace with their adversaries, which can be challenging. New antivirus technologies help organizations do so, particularly those incorporating artificial intelligence (AI) or machine learning (ML). AI/ML antivirus technologies can often detect a virus's "family" based on where they install themselves and how they remain in the network. These persistence mechanisms enable antivirus companies to use AI/ML to anticipate new variants. However, to leverage these capabilities, organizations need to configure these solutions appropriately during implementation. To create a robust ransomware mitigation program, organizations need to embrace the defense-in-depth approach, focusing on the most common vulnerabilities.

Creating a cyber-aware culture is the first step. Since most ransomware attacks rely on phishing, cyber awareness education is a key control to preventing them. Employees across all levels of the organization need to recognize, refuse, and report suspected social engineering attacks. Starting with the board of directors and senior leadership, cyber awareness education needs to be executed meaningfully, not just as a part of compliance box-checking. Organizations need to weave security into the fabric of their culture and ensure that all users understand where they fit in this process.

The second step is to use network segmentation to minimize the damage arising from a ransomware attack. With network segmentation, the organization places different data in different digital "rooms," locking each one separately. Even if malicious actors gain entrance to one room, they cannot move between them because each uses a different set of locks. For example, human resources (HR) employees can only access the network that contains their applications and data. They cannot, for example, access any network that stores the procurement department's customer payment information. Even if malicious actors steal an HR employee's credentials, they can only operate within the HR network segment. This containment prevents criminals from accessing customer payment information as well, reducing a data security event's impact.

The CISO and the board of directors: Better together

Successful CISOs communicate with their boards of directors, and successful boards of directors challenge their CISOs. To mature a company's cybersecurity posture, both CISOs and boards of directors face a learning curve to establish successful two-way communications.

A CISO needs a fully engaged board of directors that wants to understand the cybersecurity risk facing the company. The board's meeting agenda should, at minimum, include a security report so the CISO can report on any evolving risks. Additionally, a successful board engages in research and conversation with the CISO. The CISO lives and breathes the company's security risk, but board members are not employees, so they bring an outsider's viewpoint to the table. By challenging the CISO, the board can bring attention to something that a CISO may have missed and hold them accountable.

CISOs, on the other hand, need to tell a compelling story to the board. They need to find the right balance between sugarcoating the situation and giving a worst-case scenario, because neither representation is accurate on its own. If the CISO paints a rosy picture to the board but scrambles behind the scenes, the board will not understand the value of additional security investments. CISOs need to move away from technical language and focus on what their audience needs to understand. For example, instead of explaining the technical reason to patch a server, the CISO needs to explain that if a ransomware attack happens in this area of the network, a specific application will go down, affecting a given number of users. Since the board understands the business impact story, it is more likely to work with the CISO to secure the asset. Moreover, these risk narratives empower the board to ask meaningful questions and make purposeful decisions.

In a world where data security events are essentially a foregone conclusion, the board and CISO need to trust one another. Organizations looking to establish a successful, adaptive security program need cybersecurity to be a board-level corporate initiative in order to make it top of mind across the organization. Rather than shifting security leadership after an event, a successful board adapts to new risks and supports the CISO when a security event occurs, enabling them to respond appropriately, get over the immediate impact, and build out a more robust program. Two-way communication, trust building, and support act as the true differentiators for any organization looking to create a long-term, robust cybersecurity program.

Roota Almeida is the Chief Information Security Officer at Delta Dental of New Jersey and Connecticut (DDNJ, Inc.). Roota has been instrumental in helping to establish Delta Dental of New Jersey's Office of Information Security and leading the development and implementation of enterprise-wide information security strategy, policies, risk assessments and controls. She believes more women should be encouraged to pursue STEM careers and has started a summer internship program at DDNJ, Inc. specifically designed to give graduating female high school students insight into the field of corporate cybersecurity. Prior to joining Delta Dental, Roota was the Chief Information Security Officer (CISO) at Covanta Holdings Corp., a leader in Energy-from-Waste. As CISO, she led all aspects of information security and risk, including global information security awareness programs, policies, business continuity, and incident response teams. With over 15 years of direct experience in establishing and maintaining global security strategies, architectures, standards, and compliance, Roota drives the necessary cultural changes to affect measurable improvements in organizations' security posture. Roota is a recognized industry thought leader who serves as a member of the Board of Advisors at several organizations, a governing body chair for Evanta's NJ CxO Summits and other technology conferences, a faculty and a security awards judge. Her in-depth experience and expertise in the field of information security and risk management can be measured by the various articles, eBooks, interviews, and podcasts she has to her credit. Roota is also working to build and encourage new talent and solutions in the security arena. Roota holds CCISO, CISSP, CISM and CRISC certifications.

> *From a business perspective, the meaning of compliance is changing. Companies are looking at the larger, global picture.*

5

A Digital Trust Framework: A New Framework for Managing Cybersecurity

JONATHAN DAMBROT AND RIK PARKER, PRINCIPALS, KPMG

Even before the COVID-19 pandemic and resulting global economic destabilization, organizations were planning to change their approach to compliance and framework for digital trust. Traditional compliance, at the enterprise level, was outdated and broken. Companies and analysts knew this yet little innovation seemed to exist in the space.

At their core, compliance programs have straightforward functions that organizations need to fulfill. They need policies and measurements that demonstrate the organization's adherence to the appropriate policies and related controls. While that might not appear to leave room for innovation, the change in business process engineering over the past twenty years has created room for innovation. The industry itself needs to respond more effectively. In today's digitally transformed business model, IT crosses business lines, expanding from smaller teams to impact every aspect of the business. Compliance, therefore, needs a new definition to include new IT and business models, client and vendor interaction, and a digital trust framework that can adapt to the new realities.

Creating a shared definition of "compliance"

Traditionally, organizations have defined compliance as meeting the requirement for a regulatory or industry standard. However, cybersecurity and compliance professionals recognize that compliance does not equate to security. Across many data breaches, organizations have met compliance requirements yet still experienced an infiltration of their technology environments. Ultimately, this dichotomy means that companies need to go beyond the bare minimum and find a new definition of compliance.

From a business perspective, the meaning of compliance is changing. Companies are looking at the larger, global picture. Financial stability relies on customers and partnerships, and those contracts are driving mission-critical compliance requirements. Organizations now consider compliance in terms of contractual requirements, in addition to legislative and industry standards.

Business partners now require security controls as part of their contractual agreements. These requirements get pushed down further to incorporate fourth parties, ultimately applying to the upstream and downstream IT ecosystems. This new approach to compliance opens the field to innovation. CEOs look at compliance as an enabler because their business partners are starting to require continuous monitoring. Continuous monitoring may not be a regulatory requirement, but the underlying drivers help to promote stewardship, and an environment

that fosters security and compliance. This is attractive to business partners and consumers alike.

Looking forward, organizations need to pivot. They need to see compliance as part of their business operations model. They need to move away from the traditional definition of compliance and embrace the idea of compliance as creating digital trust within their revenue stream—something that begins with their customers and travels through their entire supply chain.

Adopting a digital trust framework

Conceptually, a digital trust framework starts with the business relationships that organizations already have with partners and customers, focusing on the implied social contract within these relationships. For example, every organization defines its mission statement and differentiators as part of its business goals. As customers across business-to-business and business-to-consumer channels want more security and privacy, organizations need to build capabilities into their business operations that align with those expectations, essentially creating a framework of digital trust.

The provider role's accountability for vendors' security posture is creating a higher level of security requirements than regulatory compliance. The business then focuses more on comprehensive controls rather than specific compliance requirements to protect itself and its consumers, while enabling growth objectives.

Starting with brand positioning

Building organizational direction for digital trust begins by identifying how security, privacy, and compliance fit into the organization's public-facing persona. Social media organizations, for example, may value data privacy more than certain financial institutions based on their own research into public perception. Meanwhile, if a social media account is hacked and personal information is made public, the media, private consumers, and sometimes politicians lead the call for more stringent and expansive privacy controls.

Since all brand positioning starts with knowing the customer, this acts as a perfect starting point for developing an organization's digital trust framework. Start by understanding customer or market expectations, then set security and privacy controls—including third-party risk management—aligned with those fundamental concerns.

Gaining awareness

Once the organization defines how security and privacy enable brand positioning, it must gain awareness of the digital assets that need controls. Traditional frameworks would call this "setting a risk tolerance." Still, in a digital trust framework, the organization uses the consumer as the driver rather than a disconnected law or industry standard. Awareness requires defining the data, systems, networks, devices, software, and users that interact with the information that consumers and business partners value. Fundamentally, this information is likely the same as the data that traditional security and privacy frameworks require companies to protect. However, the shift in mindset creates a more business-focused approach to placing effective controls around data confidentiality, integrity, and availability, enabling the organization to establish a "compliance-friendly" environment throughout the company.

Leveraging, and personalizing existing technology frameworks

A digital trust framework acts as a new way of thinking about what resources and assets matter, but many existing regulatory and industry-standard frameworks remain relevant to setting security controls.

Ultimately, cybersecurity programs require a foundation upon which the company can build. Organizations can start with the cybersecurity framework that makes the most sense with their organizational needs. NIST and ISO provide differing levels of prescriptive controls, but both provide a strong starting point. NIST is well recognized across industries in the US, while ISO maintains strong international support. However, organizations should also look to other industry-specific compliance requirements such as HIPAA or the FFIEC IT Manual.

To create a holistic control set, organizations need to start with a universal framework and then map additional controls from other frameworks to their needs.

Enabling CISOs to establish a digital trust framework

A digital trust framework model builds security, privacy, and compliance into an organization's business processes across department lines. However, organizations need to enable their CISOs and security teams by providing them with the right resources, authority, and risk visibility.

Helping your CISO help you

Many CISOs struggle to gain the commitment and authority necessary to secure complete, accurate data and meet compliance requirements. Despite often being held responsible for a data breach, they equally often find themselves left out of program and technology decisions. Moreover, CISOs often struggle to tell a meaningful story that senior leadership and Boards of Directors understand, unable to align tools to business defined returns on investment.

CISOs need the budget to buy the solutions that secure data, meet compliance requirements, and give the information senior leadership and Boards need. CISOs need to work to build their brand with the business leadership, generating confidence through prudent use of investments and their ability to educate stakeholders about risks in business terms.

Empowering your CISO

Empowerment is more than just dollars listed on a spreadsheet. It is about commitment to resources and to organizational cultural change. Organizations that want to maintain their competitive advantage by leveraging digital trust need senior leadership and boards to commit to the project. Digital trust relies on all business stakeholders creating a shared understanding of data's value.

A digital trust framework focuses on business relationships, including senior leadership, investors, and consumers. Empowering CISOs to meet digital trust compliance requirements means giving them the authority to make technology and program decisions. They need to be influential organizational leaders with a voice that can guide decisions impacting security and data protection. Senior leadership should trust them to communicate the necessary requirements and additional investments that may be necessary as the business changes.

Giving your CISO visibility

Giving CISOs the necessary budget and decision-making authority can help them gain the visibility needed to be successful. Every organization is another company's vendor or customer, sometimes both. To establish an effective digital trust framework, CISOs need visibility into their organizations' supply chain data security risks.

CISOs cannot diagnose problems that lead to data privacy, security, and compliance risks if they cannot see into their interconnected IT ecosystems. They need to know the potential exposures so they can effectively mitigate risk. Providing them with money and a voice does little if the organization cannot proactively view and respond to threats.

Creating trust means building relationships, internally and externally. Therefore, an effective cybersecurity and compliance program needs to start with communication. Organizations need to listen to their customers' security and privacy concerns, incorporate those into the company's primary mission, and create an internal community of leaders committed to maintaining a digital trust framework.

Rik Parker is a leading advisor in enterprise information risk management and cyber program strategy. Rik has spoken and taught globally on managing the board-level challenge of finding the right balance between business performance and the effective management of cyber risk through business aligned cyber program strategies. With 25 years of experience in cybersecurity, Rik has developed, launched, and led multiple service offerings founded on innovative thought leadership, practical transformation, and performance improvement driven through risk reduction and effective investment strategies. Rik's experience is across industries with focus areas including cyber strategy, data privacy, cyber and enterprise risk management strategies, and cyber and privacy considerations in mergers and acquisitions. Prior to KPMG, Rik led the North American Strategy and Risk practice and Global Data Privacy service offerings for another major consulting firm. In this role, he was responsible for firm-wide service strategies, go-to-market sales efforts and channel development, training programs and curriculum, and engagement delivery.

Jonathan Dambrot *is a Principal in the Cyber practice at KPMG and leads the firm's Global Third Party Security efforts. Jonathan tailors the appropriate KPMG consulting, managed services, and innovations to deliver more successful outcomes. Over the course of the last 15 years, Jonathan has worked with leading organizations in Technology, Financial Services, Energy, Life Sciences, Legal and Manufacturing to transform their 3rd party risk programs.*

Jonathan's core strength is to provide the vision, roadmap, and execution excellence to deliver the future of third-party security risk management at KPMG.

"When looking to enhance any area identified as critical to progress, start with the areas that pose the greatest risks...

6

Investing in Cybersecurity vs. Spending on Cybersecurity

**DEREK VADALA,
CEO, VISIBLERISK**

Over the last ten years, information sharing in the cybersecurity space has materially improved with CISOs now working together to share strategies for gaining business stakeholder input and support. Whether looking to industry thought leaders or engaging in peer groups, CISOs are working together more cohesively than ever, helping one another tell the stories and provide the context that elevates security dialogues beyond the technical. It's important to establish minimum standards across security domains that meet regulatory requirements and demonstrate due care. However, CISOs looking to extend and maximize cybersecurity investments need to reframe areas traditionally viewed as tactical or technical, turning them into strategic initiatives built into business processes to gain support. Areas like vulnerability management, detection and response, and employee awareness require a more holistic approach to provide the needed return on investment. Digital transformation, including the shift to cloud computing and other services-oriented technology, creates opportunities to drive new approaches (shift-left, zero-trust). To maximize return on investment as transformation occurs, a business-enabled approach to security on existing systems and processes requires a holistic approach. Security leaders need to think about the capabilities needed to succeed rather than continuing with a "need another tool" approach.

Vulnerability management

Rather than focusing primarily on scanning the enterprise for vulnerabilities, take a broader approach. Vulnerability management is the entire process of identifying vulnerabilities and defects across the ecosystem. They might appear in the organization's external attack surface, internal systems and devices, or within code developed by the organization or its suppliers.

Considered from a holistic point of view, vulnerability management includes various functional activities such as patch management, optimizing the internet attack surface, scanning, code review, penetration testing, and even red team exercises. Bringing these activities together into a comprehensive program designed to rapidly identify defects and reduce the surface area available to attackers is critical. Security leaders need to work throughout the organization to proactively build these activities into business and technology processes. These activities further enable teams throughout the organization to own and resolve issues. For example, as part of the software development lifecycle, developers should use the results of code analysis to proactively identify and fix issues before sending the application to production.

By creating an ecosystem of vulnerability management capabilities, companies can reduce risks across their connected ecosystems by further avoiding the failures we have seen drive publicly-reported cybersecurity incidents in recent years. Small improvements in these processes can significantly reduce the frequency of cyber attacks that create business impact for an organization.

Detection and response

Detection and response was historically considered a purely technical function but is now a strategic priority for security programs. Investments need to be appropriate for managing detection and response during and after a cyber event. In 2018, Crowdstrike leveraged data and generated the "1/10/60 Rule." They suggested effective organizations should "detect an intrusion in under a minute, understand it in under 10 minutes, and eject the adversary in under an hour."[1] Often, malicious actors gain access then move laterally within the company's networks until they achieve their objective—accessing

[1] Busselein, Michael. (2018). "CrowdStrike on Dark Reading: Why "Breakout Time" Is Critical to Your Security Strategy." *Crowdstrike*. May 9, 2018. https://www.crowdstrike.com/blog/crowdstrike-discusses-breakout-time-in-an-article-on-dark-reading

data, disrupting operations or perpetrating fraud. Rapid detection reduces the impact of these incidents.

Organizations may need time to build toward the key performance indicator (KPI) noted above. Focus first on a robust event management capability to ensure investigations and forensics can be performed. While this might not detect and repel an attacker, it more effectively determines impact when an incident occurs. Expand toward improving detection and alerting, set goals that measure the time it takes to respond, and then focus on processes to rapidly expel attackers from the environment. Afterward, determine impact, update key stakeholders such as regulators, board members and customers, and measure results over time.

Security event management is a core capability needed to support the activities of investigations, detecting attacks, responding rapidly to threats, and reporting incidents. Security teams need this information to effectively manage security incidents. Enrolling technology owners throughout the organization in the process enables them to implement and "feed" platforms. As the champion of these capabilities, CISOs must enroll technology teams by offering capabilities that drive improvements not directly oriented to security. For example, developers and technology operations teams can leverage log management capabilities to further their own work, such as investigating slow system performance. Exchange access to security tools for support in onboarding systems into the platform. Then, developers can think strategically about the types of events and information security teams need. This also incentivizes developers by offering capabilities they may not have the resources to acquire directly. Similarly, enterprise architects may be interested in using log information to gain visibility into shifting patterns of technology use.

After establishing base capabilities, continuously improve these processes by developing key metrics around them. The "1/10/60" rule provides a good target. Basic metrics can drive improvements. For example, measuring "dwell time," the time an attacker is in the organization undetected, gives insight into improvement areas, such as how an incident occurred, whether it could have been identified sooner, or how to respond more efficiently. One question to ask might be, "Did we discover the attack, or did someone outside our organization discover it?" If law enforcement, business partners, customers, or security researchers detected the incident first, the alert and detection process needs improvement.

Culture of security

There are many discussions on the importance of creating a "culture of security," yet articulating concrete steps for fostering one is challenging. For example, many security awareness programs focus on phishing simulations to understand failure to identify and report a potentially malicious email. Every test will have failures. In some cases, people make mistakes. Targeted, highly customized phishing campaigns fool even suspicious and well-seasoned users. Focusing on failures creates a culture of victim shaming with little connection to the underlying goal, which is to improve the organization's timeliness in responding to a real attack.

Start from the premise that successful identification tests are better indicators than failure. During a real incident, rapid reporting can make a difference between quick detection and containment versus significant impact. True educational value lies in how people apply knowledge not why they fail, which may be driven by unrelated factors such as rushing to meet a deadline or focusing on a personal issue.

After attaining a level of confidence over their workforce members' cyber hygiene, CISOs should empower people so they can make risk decisions that further reduce security friction. A classic example of this scenario is web filtering. Often, companies block access to websites, such as social media for varied reasons. Exceptions are often a high-friction process. Instead, when marketing teams need to access social media as part of their job, consider a just-in-time process of entering a business use case for immediate access. By allowing employees to provide their rationale in exchange for immediate resolution, the process reinforces risk awareness, empowering the individual making the decision. If the employee cannot articulate a business use case, they may reconsider the need.

Finally, organizational leaders need to be held to an equal level of accountability. An organization with a policy restricting access to personal email should require senior leaders to follow the rules. Creating the right culture of security requires holding everyone within the organization accountable to the same level of security awareness.

Taking purposeful action

Fundamentally, investing in these three areas can enhance security, but other capabilities may yield more effective impact for your organization. Regardless of domain, building a coalition of informed stakeholders creates empowered teams that generate results when they focus on intentional, iterative action and planning. Think holistically about how security can better enable the organization.

When looking to enhance any area identified as critical to progress, start with the areas that pose the greatest risks, whether they are business units, technologies, or processes. When thinking about vulnerability management, this might be the most critical assets, and when considering culture, it may be the highest risk users. Once identified, the organization can prioritize its investments and more appropriately determine where to apply resources. In this way, having an intentional approach can help reduce risk more efficiently.

Collaboration and communication

Any area of investment requires coalition building. CISOs need to build programs, enroll stakeholders, and effectively communicate results—positive or otherwise—to business executives in a way that demystifies the discipline's technical side. Moving from the tactical to the strategic requires organizational investments in tools that enable stakeholder knowledge sharing and collaboration, which will lead to a more robust security posture that mitigates threats. Furthermore, empowering end users with risk decision-making means giving them tools that allow them to communicate their reasoning and work with security teams. Fundamentally, cybersecurity relies on information sharing and collaboration to create a holistic, mature program.

No single approach or program focus will fit every organization, but considering some of these fundamental problem-solving approaches can help teams think about investing in capabilities rather than simply spending on more tools.

Derek Vadala is the CEO of VisibleRisk, a joint venture between Moody's Corporation, a global integrated risk assessment firm, and Team8, a cybersecurity-focused company creation platform. Derek leads a team that is focused on creating a standard benchmark for communicating cyber risk to Boards of Directors and senior business executives in order to improve the global dialog about this important issue. Prior to leading this venture, Derek was the Global Head of Cyber Risk for Moody's Investors Service, responsible for developing capabilities for evaluating cyber risk and incorporating those capabilities into credit analysis. Prior to that, Derek served as the Chief Information Security Officer for Moody's Corporation from 2013-2018, where he was responsible for global information risk and security across Moody's businesses worldwide.

> **"**
> *Cyber risk is everywhere. Increasingly, cyber insurance is no longer simply 'off the shelf.'*

7

Cyber Insurance: What to Look For and What to Spend

ANTHONY DAGOSTINO, EXECUTIVE VP, GLOBAL CYBER AND TECHNOLOGY PRACTICE LEADER, LOCKTON COMPANIES

When organizations engage in their cyber risk assessment process, they face important decisions around whether to accept, refuse, mitigate, or transfer risk. A decade ago, cyber risk insurance might only have been considered by Fortune 500 companies because their digital footprint and amount of data held made them prime targets. With digital transformation, cybercriminals now target organizations of all sizes. This makes cyber risk insurance as important to continued financial stability as general liability and property policies. However, for organizations to feel confident when seeking cyber risk insurance, they need to understand how their coverage matches with their operations, and how to quantify risks. They need to understand a bad day in cybersecurity just as they understand it for other lines of insurance.

The top three cyber insurance myths

Although companies know that cyber insurance offers them a way to protect against the inevitable data security incident, many senior executives and directors hold misconceptions around the product. News outlets report coverage litigation but fail to acknowledge the times when cyber insurance worked. Ultimately, this reporting gap leaves decision-makers wary. Here are the top three myths and realities of cyber insurance.

Myth #1: It doesn't work

Reality: Cyber risk insurance policies focus on risks directly tied to information and data security events.

Behind every coverage litigation lies a story. In the cyber risk insurance world, most policies work and insurance companies pay the claims. However, the instances that make headlines often involve outdated policy terms or non-cyber policies, like property policies with a cyber "rider." Riders typically customize a policy with benefits generally considered outside the original scope.

In recent years, one newsworthy coverage litigation illuminates the reason that companies need to purchase designated cyber insurance policies. In the aftermath of the NotPetya data breach, an insured brought a claim under the cyber risk rider in its property policy. The insurance company denied coverage citing the war exclusion. Traditional property and general liability policies with riders do not adequately address cybersecurity risks.

Myth #2: It doesn't cover anything

Reality: Coverage exclusions focus on a limited activity set mostly

related to an insured's malicious intent. Also, in some cases, an insured can purchase additional coverage that is otherwise excluded.

At first glance, the long list of policy exclusions appears to negate coverage for nearly every use case. From a high level, a policy may have twenty-six or more exclusions. However, companies can pay for additional coverage based on their individual needs.

In 2019, the *Journal of Cybersecurity* published a paper titled, "Content analysis of cyber insurance policies: how do carriers price cyber risk?"[1] The authors noted that common exclusions focused primarily on "criminal, fraudulent, or dishonest acts, errors, omissions, intentional violation of a law, any ongoing criminal investigation or proceedings,

---

[1] Romanosky, Sasha, Lilian Ablon, Andreas Kuehn, and Therese Jones. (2019). "Content analysis of cyber insurance policies: how do carriers price cyber risk?" *Journal of Cybersecurity*. https://clearwatercompliance.com/wp-content/uploads/2019/10/Content-analysis-of-cyber-insurance-policies-how-do-carriers-price-cyber-risk.pdf

and payment of fines, penalties, or fees."[2]

The research listed the following as the ten most common exclusions:
- Criminal or fraudulent act
- Negligent disregard for computer security
- Loss to system not owned or operated
- Bodily injury
- Contractual liability
- Act of terrorism, war, military action
- Act of God
- IP theft
- Seizure or destruction of system by government
- Fines, penalties, fees

Myth #3: It's only for data breaches and digital data

Reality: Coverage under cyber risk policies is not limited to digital information, it can also include spoken and paper communications.

Many companies believe that because the term "cyber" is in the policy type, it only covers data breaches and digital information. Just as scanning through exclusions creates misconceptions, so does browsing through insuring agreements' bold titles. Traditional insuring agreements provide coverage for:
- Loss of digital assets
- Non-physical business interruption
- Cyber extortion threat
- Security event costs

[2] *Ibid.*

- Network security and privacy
- Employee privacy
- Electronic media
- Cyber terrorism

Customers should read the long list of definitions to gain a better perspective of their policies. For example, some policies define "personally identifiable information" to include identifiers *whether in electronic or paper format.*

Myth #4: It's too expensive, and it can't be priced well
Reality: Organizations of any size can find an appropriately priced, affordable insurance policy.

Five or more years ago, pricing cyber risk policies was problematic due to a lack of necessary data sets. Often, the questions underwriters asked were in binary "yes or no" form, such as whether the insured used encryption. However, as the industry processes more claims and gains better insight into data security incident costs, the market firmed up.

Today, insurance companies use data analytics to weigh responses and supplement pricing with tools like security ratings platforms. In fact, over the last two years, security ratings platforms and other non-intrusive external monitoring tools have become a market standard.

Cyber risk insurance considerations
To appropriately transfer risk using a cyber insurance policy, organizations need to start by planning. The only way to transfer risk is to know the risks the business faces and understand the services necessary to protect from them.

Knowing what's critical

As part of a company's compliance program, it needs to identify, analyze, and assess risk. They can start by using this analysis as a baseline, but also need to consider:

- How many employees are there?
- How many customers are there?
- What would happen if malicious actors hacked the company?
- What would happen if an insider stole business-critical information?

Potential long-term impact

Data breaches can have long-tail impacts. After the initial discovery and notification, many companies experience financial and reputational repercussions. Data breaches will continue to happen, despite a company's best efforts. Organizations need to consider some of the following questions:

- What is the five-year impact that a data incident will have on customer churn?
- What is the five-year impact that a data incident will have on stock prices?
- What is the five-year impact that a data breach will have on expenses that undercut revenue?

Understanding incident response maturity

Depending on a company's size, it may need to include incident response as part of the insurance package. Some companies lack the security staff necessary to manage the incident response themselves. Others have a more mature program with enough staff to manage the response, which creates conflict with the insurance company. In some cases, a policyholder may want the insurance company to provide the law firm that handles notification and forensics.

When considering a cyber risk policy, companies should analyze the following:

- What level of staffing is necessary to respond rapidly?
- What relationships does the organization already have that it would want to use for incident response?
- How much involvement does the company want to have in the response process?

Communicating with the broker

Unlike insurance agents who work for the insurance company, the broker acts as a policyholder's partner. Insurance brokers can help companies better understand the amount of risk they need to transfer. Some questions to ask the broker include:

- How much insurance is necessary to meet contractual requirements and actual risk?
- How do the exclusions impact the risk transferred?
- Does the policy cover trade secrets?
- Will the incident response coverage adequately protect the organization?

Understanding additional services

Many insureds do not know that cyber risk insurers often provide additional services. Like an annual preventive physical exam covered by a health insurer, cyber insurers include services that lower a company's risk. Some examples of these services include:

- Phishing attack simulations
- Mock cyber attack exercises
- Free assessment tools

Cyber risk is everywhere

Data is an important asset that every organization needs to protect. In today's modern world, information touches every business process across every industry. Cybersecurity is no longer solely the domain of IT departments. The entire executive suite and board of directors needs to understand cyber risk to mitigate or transfer it effectively.

Cyber risk is everywhere. Increasingly, cyber insurance is no longer simply "off the shelf." Other lines of coverage include elements of cyber risk, but that is changing as insurance companies look to limit their cyber exposure across multiple policies. From business interruption and property to directors' and officers' coverage, many types of policies contain an element of cyber risk. However, creating a patchwork of coverage still leaves organizations at risk. The only way to fully transfer cybersecurity risk is to create an appropriately tailored cyber risk policy that meets the company's needs.

Anthony Dagostino is executive vice president and Global Cyber & Technology Practice leader for Lockton, the world's largest privately held, independent insurance broker and consultant. Anthony oversees Lockton's cyber strategy focusing on delivering innovative and effective solutions to clients across the globe through risk transfer solutions, analytics and risk consulting. Prior to joining Lockton in July 2019, he led Willis Towers Watson's global cyber risk consulting and insurance brokerage practices. He brings nearly two decades of experience in cyber, technology, and financial lines insurance underwriting and brokerage through an array of leadership positions. Prior to joining the insurance industry, Anthony was a research analyst in the venture capital space focusing on early-stage emerging technology companies. Anthony serves on numerous advisory boards helping start-up companies and also participates in various public-private sector working groups. He is a regular contributor to news media and is active in his hometown community through a number of charities.

> **"**
>
> *CISOs may not have troops in the field, but they are dealing with constant conflict, attempted invasions, and attacks.*

8

Operating in Wartime

RAY MABUS, FORMER SECRETARY OF THE U.S. NAVY, CURRENT CEO, MABUS GROUP

I was sworn in as Secretary of the Navy on the afternoon of May 19th, 2009. It became a nonstop 24-hour job, because people's lives could depend on the decisions that I was being called upon to make. The job started the instant I put my hand down while being sworn in and didn't end until I left on January 20th, 2017.

That constant state of vigilance is what's called a "wartime mentality." It's a mindset that will be familiar to any good Chief Information Security Officer (CISO), because whether they know it or not, they're also in the business of war.

What is a wartime mentality?

A wartime mentality means that you never have downtime, can never relax, can never rest on your laurels. You never get to cross the goal line and spike the ball. It's a conflict, and it's an ongoing, never-ending conflict.

I spent 26 years in the public service as, among other things, a governor, ambassador and Secretary of the Navy, but I also spent years in the private business sector. I've been on seven different public boards and several more private boards. I was CEO of a public company from 2006 to 2007 and had to deal with a public board and all the requirements that went with a public board. I was chairman of that company for five years, Today I am on three public boards. One of the things I've learned in my career is that the public and private sectors often overlap, especially in the issues they face.

Cyber is a new field of warfare. In the military, it's becoming as important as—or perhaps more important than—sea, air, or land. At the Pentagon, Cyber Command is now a combat command on the same level as geographic commands such as European Command and Indo-Pacific Command. That cyber is now considered a wartime command illustrates cyber's importance to the Pentagon, as not many new fields of warfare get their own combat command. This designation is justified, however. When Russia invaded Ukraine, their opening salvos were massive cyber attacks. Increasingly, the mastery of cyber, both defensively and offensively, is the crucial element in potential conflicts.

CISOs may not have troops in the field, but they are dealing with constant conflict, attempted invasions, and attacks. Except for potential loss of life—and that's a big exception—the threats faced by CISOs are more or less the same as those faced by the military. Sometimes the enemies are also the same people, and many times the aims of their attacks are the same: spreading confusion and disinformation, or gaining information. And of course, in the private sector, so often the goal is just plain stealing money.

For this reason, CISOs are at war 24 hours a day. There's never a let-up,

there's never a pause, and there's never a time when people aren't trying to compromise your countermeasures, or infiltrate your networks using automated tools that allow for an infinite number of attacks.

How can CISOs cultivate a wartime mentality?

In cybersecurity, the adversary is always evolving. They're always using different tools or different tricks, changing their weapons, and tweaking their tactics to target whatever your vulnerabilities are—and those vulnerabilities shift over time.

A CISO must do exactly the same thing. They cannot just be goalies, keeping people out. They must also be attackers who use new tools and strategies to get ahead of attackers and proactively block attacks before they happen.

An important thing to understand here is that like a military official, a CISO can't do all of this alone. They need people around them who can help, who bring diverse experiences and opinions, and a range of expertise to a security team.

This is one of the reasons that I pushed so hard for a diverse force in the Navy, repealing Don't Ask, Don't Tell, bringing ROTC to very diverse campuses and back to Ivy League schools, and opening all jobs to women in the Navy and the Marines. If a military force looks too much alike and comes from the same backgrounds, they become predictable, and a predictable military force is a defeatable military force. It's the same in corporate America. If you don't have a diverse workforce, if everybody looks the same, if everybody comes from the same background and thinks alike, you're going to be in trouble, because you're going to miss important details in cybersecurity and in other areas as well. Part of a wartime mentality is getting all the information you can.

Getting good intelligence is also important, and a big part of a good cybersecurity is good intel. A CISO needs to know where the criminals are spending time online, what the new attack modes are, and what tools are being used. CISOs should be aware of attacks that have happened in their sector, and how those attacks were carried out so they can test their defenses against that vulnerability.

Lastly, CISOs need good tools that give them visibility into their vulnerabilities and those of their partners and vendors.

Adaptability is a critical part of the wartime mentality

When I was Secretary of the Navy, I used to sit in on the debriefings of carrier strike teams who had been on eight and nine month deployments. There was only one constant in each debriefing: the group had always faced an obstacle they had not expected, or trained for. They just had to figure it out while the incident was happening.

Being a CISO today is probably one of the hardest jobs there is because it's never-ending, and the work you do is only measurable in the negative. If there aren't any breaches, you're not called in and given a trophy If there is an incident, you are called in and you're not getting a trophy. A CISO's greatest virtue is flexibility, not deciding you've got all the answers.

Planning, although you should do it, won't always prevent every obstacle. To quote Mike Tyson, "everybody's got a plan until they get punched in the mouth."

The biggest mistake a CISO can make is to think that a snapshot, which is what we're doing today, is anything but a snapshot. If things are going well now, that doesn't mean you're going to be doing that well tomorrow, or next week, or two months from now. You've got to remain able to pivot, you've got to remain able to go after new threats, and you can't wait until that threat comes to you.

Ray Mabus has been Secretary of the US Navy, Governor, Ambassador and CEO. Mabus served as the 75th United States Secretary of the Navy from 2009 to 2017, the longest tenure as leader of the Navy and Marine Corps since World War I. As Secretary during President Obama's Administration, he revolutionized the Navy and Marine Corps, opening all jobs to women, aggressively moving to alternative energy as a warfighting measure, building more than twice as many ships during his term than in the preceding eight years and developing the Gulf Coast Restoration Plan after the Deepwater Horizon oil spill. It was during his watch that Navy SEALs killed Osama bin Laden. Among many awards, he was chosen as one of the top fifty CEOs in America by GlassDoor, the only government person picked. From 1988 to 1992, Mabus served as Governor of Mississippi, the youngest elected to that office in more than 150 years. Mississippi experienced record growth in jobs, education, tourism and exports.

Mabus was United States Ambassador to the Kingdom of Saudi Arabia from 1994-1996. He was CEO of a public company from 2006-2007 leading it out of bankruptcy in less than a year while paying all creditors in full and saving equity. Today, Mabus is Chairman of InStride, a public benefit education company, a director of three public companies, Hilton and Dana, the founder of Mabus Group, a consulting organization, an executive fellow at Harvard Business School and board member or advisor to several other companies. He is a member of the Council on Foreign Relations, the Explorers Club, and the Screen Actors Guild. He serves on the boards of the Environmental Defense Fund and Jose Andreas' World Central Kitchen. He has thrown out the first pitch at all 30 major league ballparks. He has stood on both poles and, during his life, has traveled to more than 190 countries and territories.

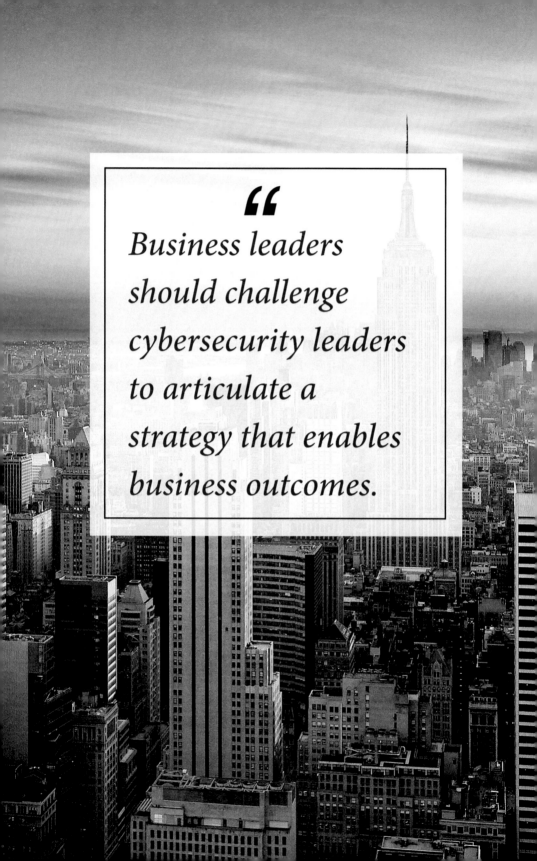

"

Business leaders should challenge cybersecurity leaders to articulate a strategy that enables business outcomes.

9

Shifting the Perception of Security From Cost Center

BRIAN CINCERA, SVP & CHIEF INFORMATION SECURITY OFFICER, PFIZER, INC.

"Hope is not a strategy." – James Cameron

Since the early days of the dot com era, cybersecurity professionals have predicted and hoped that customers would pay a premium for great security. Although not a crazy idea, nearly a quarter century later, it has not yet materialized. Customers the world over pay extra for great packaging, better performance, or brand prestige, but steadfastly expect that protection of transactions, personal information, financial records, consumption habits, and communications are inherently included. This reality, combined with increasing consumer protection regulations, leaves companies in most industries unable to turn security investments into top- and bottom-line financial gains. The business case for cybersecurity is that smart investments protect revenue, profit, and reputation. Business leaders and boards of directors should expect that cybersecurity program expenditures are appropriate for the risk reducing benefits they generate. This expectation implies a clear-eyed accounting of where resources are being applied and a reasonable quantification of the beneficial outcomes achieved. Business leaders should challenge cybersecurity leaders to articulate a strategy that enables business outcomes, just as it helps assure those outcomes are reasonably protected from the foreseeable threats of operating in the digital age.

The best cybersecurity programs meet this investment-to-risk-reduction challenge by focusing on three key elements: balanced resource allocation, efficiency, and talent management.

Balance

Organizations must balance the allocation of limited resources between preventing security incidents, quickly detecting those that cannot be prevented, and responding decisively to minimize disruption and financial loss.

Prevention

An ounce of prevention is worth a pound of cure, or so the saying goes. Cybersecurity programs rightly allot the largest proportion of their security budget to preventative measures designed to stop attack attempts from becoming breaches.

The cybersecurity technology landscape is a minefield of mostly niche firms with specialty hardware and software, each designed to prevent relatively narrow types of attacks. Many address esoteric threats that should rightly be low on the priority list for most firms. Many cybersecurity prevention technologies are wildly expensive with both obvious and hidden costs, like hardware and software, storage,

networking, upkeep, maintenance, and tuning labor. They generate reams of alerts about potential threats that leave cybersecurity teams struggling to prioritize the highest risks. Ultimately, companies that chase the latest tech can find themselves buried under increasing costs without dramatically reducing operational risk.

The best programs focus meaningful resources on basic protections like securing devices, networks, and applications, as well as implementing practices like quickly patching risky vulnerabilities, scanning internet-connected devices regularly, and verifying the security of deployments before they go into production. These basic practices are not particularly expensive, but collectively, they generate meaningful risk reduction.

When looking to balance cost with benefit, solutions that manage these fundamental practices offer the most value for the dollar.

Rapid detection

No level of prevention can successfully defend every attack. Cybersecurity defenders are confronted with active adversaries who are looking for newer, better, and more creative ways of compromising those defenses. In the same way that business leaders face hard-working, creative competitors in the marketplace, the lucrative nature of cybercrime underpins an endless arms race.

Seasoned cybersecurity detection capabilities seek to identify attacks early in this progression of steps, offering the opportunity to take mitigating actions before damage is done. One of the greatest challenges is that the digitization of business is generating an unfathomable quantity to data to be analyzed. Many organizations face millions to billions of telemetry data points, within which are the "signals" they are attempting to find.

The challenges of detection may be the best use of advanced analytics and data science. Security professionals have developed thousands of detection techniques, and there is a growing range of artificial intelligence technologies to help defenders find attack signals in the sea of noise.

Decisive response

Some of the most notable failures in cybersecurity have not been that an attack was successful, but instead how the response was managed. No one knows when attacks will happen, which ones will succeed, or how badly they will hurt. However, it is clear that the time to plan and organize response capabilities is not during a crisis.

The best cybersecurity leaders learn from their own near misses and the mishaps of others. They plan for a wide range of potential impacts, from financial losses, to operational outages, to reputational damage. They also plan that during extraordinary times, basic capabilities like email, organization charts, phone service, user authentication, physical building control systems, online meeting services, and access to disaster recovery plans may be compromised.

Like military units, effective incident response teams also routinely conduct practice drills to assure that plans on paper can withstand real-life pressures. The best drill scenarios engage business leaders and staff, and they confront a wide range of challenges that teams frequently face. These include determining who is in charge, where decision rights start and stop, how to rotate staff during prolonged events, how to manage inevitable inquiries from the media, and how to communicate effectively during the crisis in ways that limit exposure during the nearly inevitable post-event litigation.

Ruthless efficiency

Delivering return on investment requires extracting efficiencies from cybersecurity program expenditures. A sad reality for cyber defenders is that attack methods and malicious viruses never disappear. As new attacker techniques emerge, they are simply added to the ever-growing list. None are ever fully retired.

Leaders must constantly extract more capability from people and past technology investments. Using process automation and machine analytics increases efficiency, but so do more classic approaches, like implementing automation or other improvement programs that eliminate errors or duplicative effort. Cybersecurity programs that prove efficiency gains will more easily defend their cost in relation to their return.

Talent strategy

An essential element of managing risk-reducing return is to win the battle for talent. According to *Cybersecurity Ventures*, "there will be 3.5 million unfilled cybersecurity jobs globally by 2021, up from one million positions in 2014."[1] Those with cyber talent can bid up salaries, and the richest firms seem like the only winners. Creative recruitment strategies and continuing education are low-cost ways to bring in the right talent. Great leaders cultivate long-term, happy, productive employees rather than buying them. Cyber professionals frequently flourish in job rotation programs, while expanding their experience and building company loyalty. Investing in employee education broadens the cybersecurity program's depth and reduces long-term new-hire costs.

Programs that recruit talent in high school or junior high school community programs by offering summer internships can lead to full-time roles after graduation. Military veterans frequently bring deep discipline and commitment to mission to cyber jobs, and a number of non-profit education programs are dedicated to assisting veterans with the transition to civilian work.

Finally, cybersecurity overwhelmingly skews male and white, to its own detriment. It is imperative that the industry take more active steps to engage women and underrepresented communities if it is to foster a growing, healthy and engaged workforce. Building talent in house requires an investment in education, but leads to long-term employee retention and a return on that investment.

Risk reduction on investment

Business leaders and boards of directors are justified in continuing to ask if cybersecurity investment levels are appropriate and returning sufficient results. The following guideposts are worthy of consideration.

Spend metrics like cybersecurity expense as a percentage of revenue or as a percentage of IT expense are common and easy to create, although crude. These categories of spending metrics lack context

---

[1] Morgan, Steve. (2019) "Cybersecurity Talent Crunch To Create 3.5 Million Unfilled Jobs Globally By 2021." *Cybersecurity Ventures*. October 24, 2019. https://cybersecurityventures.com/jobs/

around how operators account for costs, frequently excluding buried infrastructure and compliance cost savings that generate beneficial returns. Absolute benchmark comparisons fail because threat realities vary widely. However, determining whether a program wildly deviates from a spending benchmark offers value.

Although far more intangible, organizational risk tolerance provides greater visibility into ROI. Nearly all business leaders accept some level of operational outage as a fact of life. Many organizations are beginning to quantify cyber risk by measuring likelihood and impact using methods similar to other loss events like storm damage or automobile accidents. Any resource allocation approach should include at least annual reviews of current and emerging perils, the depth and quality of mitigation programs, and some quantification of the residual cyber risk the organization is willing to accept.

Finally, every industry sector has a non-profit security community sharing entity called an Information Sharing and Analysis Center (ISAC), originally created by a presidential executive order. They aim to connect sector participants to share security best practices and techniques in a non-competitive manner. With low or non-existent member dues for not-for-profit entities and small businesses, ISACs deliver extensive opportunities to learn from others, share techniques, find staff looking for new opportunities, or get help with an immediate issue. The high return from ISAC membership and active participation makes it a "must have" investment for any cybersecurity program.

Like all risk management efforts, some bad outcomes are inevitable in spite of best efforts. Businesses that take no risk should expect no profits. Cybersecurity programs that attempt to eliminate every risk inevitably stifle business innovation. Great programs that enable business outcomes measure performance to assure meaningful return on investments, thoroughness of key protection deployments, detection and response speed, cyber drill outcomes, and number of repeat incidents. Each of these help business leaders, directors, and cybersecurity professionals evaluate the effectiveness of their resource allocation decisions.

Brian Cincera has global responsibility for Pfizer's enterprise infrastructure, multi-cloud platforms, IT operations and information security technology and risk management capabilities. In his role, Brian oversees strategy development, technology operations and infrastructure services delivery at more than 500 Pfizer locations. As part of Pfizer's Enterprise Risk Management program, Brian is responsible for leading its information security risk governance process including regular reporting to Pfizer's executive leadership and Board of Directors. Prior to his current role, Brian led a wide range of technology teams in both infrastructure and cybersecurity, including strategic leadership for a wide range of enterprise-wide deployment programs. He joined Pfizer in 2005 after working with the company to develop its digital credential and electronic identity strategy. Before joining Pfizer, Brian worked at Greenwich Technology Partners, Bolt Baranek & Newman (BBN) and other strategic security consulting firms supporting the Financial Services, Telecommunications, Transportation and Energy industries, inside and outside of the United States. Brian is the Board Chairman for the Health Information Sharing and Analysis Center (H-ISAC), the Department of Homeland Security affiliated entity for enhancing cybersecurity across the healthcare sector. Brian holds a Bachelor of Science in Business Administration from Penn State University and lives in Allentown, PA with his wife and two school-age daughters.

> **"**
> *Organizations need to invest in creative people with frontline cybersecurity teams and control methods experience.*

10

Thinking Outside the Compliance Box: Creating Innovative Security Programs

MORIAH HARA, HEAD OF CYBERSECURITY & TECHNOLOGY RISK, BMO FINANCIAL GROUP

How can highly regulated companies stay innovative in their security and risk programs if they need to invest significant energy toward the deluge of audits, regulator exams and control assessments?

Cybersecurity attack techniques and threat actors move faster than regulations and industry standards can be updated. Therefore, companies need an innovative, proactive approach to security, risk, and compliance that moves at the pace of the adversary. Simultaneously, companies need to meet new business challenges, expand their digital footprints in response to customer expectations, and "check the boxes" required by strict compliance mandates. A look at these highly regulated industries explains the reason for the rigid compliance mandates. Whether critical infrastructure, government, financial services, or healthcare; they all collect, transmit, store, and process extremely sensitive data, making them prime targets for malicious actors.

Creative security and compliance programs focus on risk

Compliance "boxes" exist to make sure risk managers consider everything that could go wrong. The compliance box is a safe place for many financial organizations and others in highly-regulated industries. Companies worry about regulators and audit teams finding noncompliance issues against the required framework or control set. While audit teams can be more focused on processes that enable compliance, regulators look for companies to proactively address emerging risks and concerns.

Thinking "outside the compliance box" takes extra effort. Organizations need to invest in creative people with frontline cybersecurity teams and control methods experience. They need people who understand how to take a risk-based approach that prioritizes allocating scarce resources to the highest-impact risk areas. To uncover key risks, these teams must find the 'needle in the haystack' amongst the constant stream of risk intelligence, while consuming hundreds of findings across their self-assessments, audits, security incidents, and regulator issuances—while also looking at future threat trends.

Finally, connecting with industry peers to share best practices and threat events is critical to uncovering new risks. Regardless of industry, companies that want to prevent incidents in their environments benefit from sharing intelligence with risk peers. Threat actors constantly leverage new techniques to skirt corporate security walls. A unique attack against one industry member is likely to hit others.

For example, as CISO at Interpublic Group, I spearheaded the first media- and advertising-industry CISO intel sharing forum, which approached and resolved common vendor and industry problems. The group generated better overall results than any single firm alone could have managed. Across industries, most competitors do not allow their teams to talk to each other, but are comfortable with their risk teams sharing cybersecurity risk information when looking to fight against the same fraudsters and attackers.

Fundamentally, organizations in highly-regulated industries want to drive smart spending on targeted investments in high-risk areas that effectively manage cyber and technology risk aligned to critical business assets. The objective of the compliance boxes is preventing significant negative events from impacting the company. Taking a risk-driven approach that sees the big picture, and allocates limited resources to the most prescient risks, can both minimize risk to the company and win the confidence of regulators and customers.

Security innovation in highly-regulated industries

An 'innovative' security solution closely aligns with the changing business and technology trends that companies are embracing in this accelerated digital era. Innovation requires making decisions based on capabilities—not just packaging new trends.

Leverage artificial intelligence (AI) and machine learning (ML)

While AI and ML promise to process data and apply analytics at a much more rapid pace than human teams can, organizations must be able to measure their effectiveness. As an example, improved automation, and data analytics applied to security analytics and infrastructure protection, offer to find more attacks, reduce false alerts, and perform faster detect-and-respond functions. But to do it right, companies need data science experts to vet these solutions.

Key considerations include:

- How to view/control your data that the solution uses
- Whether the solutions send your data outside the organization
- How the vendor protects this data
- Relevant security and performance metrics to prove AI's value to the program
- Peer reviews of the solution
- Staff and time required to maintain the solution
- Solution's ability to integrate into enterprise workflow
- Solution's integrations with GRC and other tools and applications
- Where the solution gets the data signals it uses

Security and risk leaders should take the lead in establishing what the organization requires and how AI can assist in that. Companies should also set reasonable expectations for what AI can realistically provide, and select projects based on areas where AI can have the greatest impact.

Partner with security company start-ups

Partnering with start-ups and early-stage security companies can provide insight into the most innovative solutions and talent in the industry, enabling a creative approach to solve the biggest or newest risk challenges. Quite a few of the largest retail and investment banks in the country have dedicated resources assigned to evaluating, piloting, and potentially investing in innovative security solutions. Providing feedback on an early-growth company's roadmap can help address a current gap within the organization and build the ecosystem. Many security leaders complain that getting an established vendor to innovate is like getting an oil tanker to turn. Early-stage and start-up cybersecurity firms provide program and technology agility.

Personalization

With start-ups, CISOs can influence the product's roadmap by advocating for features that suit their organization's unique security needs. Start-ups lack the bureaucracy of established vendors, giving CISOs the opportunity to have their voices heard by forging relationships with senior management. This relationship helps smooth out the inevitable bumps in the road. Established vendors often lack this personalized experience because they manage a multitude of customer requirements on their roadmaps.

Agility

Organizations can move faster and have greater flexibility with early-stage cybersecurity firms. Without the red tape, early-stage firms can move more quickly to pivot their technology. From inception to prototype, they are unencumbered by legacy technical debt, allowing them to act more rapidly. Thus, the CISO can shape the solution's roadmap to meet their needs and have it done more rapidly.

Influence

Less obviously, the features co-created with the early-stage cybersecurity firms can influence the entire industry, possibly changing the industry approach in the start-up's area. Partnering can enable CISOs to deliver business value faster and remain ahead of the curve. For example, one CISO indicated that they could deliver their services more quickly and, in some cases, had also removed a lot of cost from how their team delivers security to their organization. Reviewing innovative security solutions can keep a company's security program ahead of the curve by giving an early look at the industry's responses to newly identified problems.

Creating an effective partnership

CISOs need to create a plan if they want to work with start-ups and early-stage cybersecurity firms. The plan should include:

- Providing strategic focus areas
- Prioritizing the security team's review of emerging technology
- Formally assigning this responsibility to a team member
- Establishing an innovation fund that bypasses organizational inertia to drive proofs of concept and solution testing in the environment

Establishing an integrated, innovative security and compliance program

Every organization should be looking to establish a security compliance program as innovative as the organization's business goals. In a digitally transformed world, being forward thinking in business requires a similar future-forward focus on mitigating security and compliance risk. To do this, senior leadership, risk management, and security leaders must work as a team.

Gaining continuous visibility

Continuous risk intelligence monitoring is key. Risk teams in the first or second line of defense need to identify the right risk indicators (KRI's) by tracking what is most critical. This can be done by having a continually refreshed set of KRI's and Key Performance Indicators (KPIs) with thresholds to call out when high risk patterns appear. Leveraging data analytics and other automated tools helps support the business by identifying pertinent risk triggers. With predictive analytics, organizations can align their security and compliance postures more effectively and take a future-focused risk management approach that ultimately reduces audit and regulatory findings, as well as security incidents.

Leveraging collaboration tools

Feeding issues into a central risk management platform is critical to giving teams the integrated and accurate view of risk intelligence they need to make the right decisions. With a centralized risk management platform enabling more cohesive collaboration, organizations can realize the unified vision. They need a single, authoritative source of risk documentation–past, present, and predicted-future–to see patterns as they emerge. Past findings need to be applied to current-state processes and operations. All of this needs to be aligned with predictive risk triggers so that organizations can continuously iterate based on data.

Focusing on governance

Many organizations use customized frameworks to manage their security controls. Staff typically only review these controls frameworks quarterly or annually, viewing them as a checkmark for the compliance box. Ideally, they should switch to a governance process that lets them perform continuous monitoring of controls. Creativity and innovation require evaluation and response to emerging risk patterns. A governance-focused security and compliance program shifts from following possibly outdated compliance requirements, to proactively managing emerging risks shown to have a high impact on the success of the security program.

Moriah Hara is currently Head of Cybersecurity & Technology Risk, BMO Financial Group that is a diversified financial services provider based in North America with total assets of $709 billion. Moriah holds enterprise accountability for leading the second line of defense function responsible for providing critical and independent oversight for cybersecurity, technology, fraud, physical security and emerging risks such as Cloud, data, AI and data & analytics. Moriah brings over 20 years of experience in leading large-scale cybersecurity and cyber risk transformations across financial institutions as a CISO at Wells Fargo Capital Markets and as Global CISO at the Interpublic group. She won the ISE North East CISO Executive of the Year in 2019. She is also an advisor, mentor and employer to urban young adults through the 'Year Up' program in NYC and teaches cybersecurity for girl scout badges. Moriah has been widely recognized for her domain expertise and was named as one of the top 100 Fascinating Women Fighting Cyber by Cybercrime Magazine, and is a sought-after thought leader at security forums such as FS-ISAC, FINRA, SINET, and Bloomberg publications. Moriah received her BS from Strayer University, Magna Cum Laude and is a graduate of Harvard University's Executive Cybersecurity Program.

> **"**
> *The number one piece of advice I'd give any CISO new to the job is to first build relationships.*

11

S: The Secrets CISOs Keep

SAM KASSOUMEH, COO AND CO-FOUNDER, SECURITYSCORECARD

Once viewed as another department in IT, the role of the CISO has been elevated, as it is now clear that information security cannot be left out of any conversation about organizational resilience or business continuity management. But what are the secrets to being a great CISO?

Secret #1: Strength Comes from Weakness

You can find strength in weakness, which seems counterintuitive to being a CISO. What that means is avoid reporting everything as green or in good health. If you report transparently on what's not working, it can quickly empower you to improve the cyber resilience of your organization more swiftly. You can actually make a business case when things are not good. For example, if someone has an 'F' on SecurityScorecard, you can go to the board and your CFO and leverage that to get a budget to fix it.

Secret #2: Speed Brings Success

Make an immediate impactful change by finding a quick win. Executing quickly and demonstrating momentum will build trust in the security function and yield returns in the long run. Making security a department that can be trusted to move fast with precision can lead to proud moments for a CISO and for the company as a whole. Seeing that the controls you put in place are stopping or preventing a very serious incident from occurring is one of the most gratifying feelings. Catching vulnerabilities before they go to production is a moment to be proud of. Your efforts can also make a material impact on the business, like helping a deal get done faster because of good, healthy cybersecurity hygiene and the controls that were put in place. Finally, when a cyber hacker or fraudster gets caught because of work that you did, that feels good.

Secret #3: Building a Culture of Security Is the Most Powerful Tool in Your Arsenal

A culture of security is as powerful, if not more so, than the security controls themselves. Building a security-minded culture on day one inside a company will help help the medicine go down easier. To succeed in building an effective culture around cybersecurity, you've got to work top-down, and bottom-up simultaneously.

Top-down means you go right to the board, to the CEO, and to the non-technical executive team, and you get their buy-in on promoting cybersecurity across the company.
An effective buy-in conversation would go something like this:
You: "Do you like bad events and breaches?"
Them: "No."

You: "Do you want bad events and breaches to happen?"
Them: "Of course not."
You: "I'm here to help protect against those things. I'm looking to keep the company safe and out of trouble."

The key is to get heads nodding and unite the room. Then you tell them that all cybersecurity efforts need to be a unified effort. This way, when you roll out security measures like having everybody change their passwords every 90 days, even though everybody grumbles the executives know it's necessary to make the company cyber secure. Your security efforts will have full support from the top down.

Bottom-up means things like doing security awareness training, contests, or hackathons. You could also conduct a security championship award program that gets peers at all levels of the company interested and engaged in fun ways to understand what cybersecurity means and why it's important. Everybody in the organization can be a promoter of cybersecurity.

The number one piece of advice I'd give any CISO new to the job is to first build relationships with the executive team, make everyone in the organization aware that you're here to make change, and educate the business about why you're here and what you're here to do.

Secret #4: Get Comfortable with Some People Being Uncomfortable

Typically, cybersecurity is the enemy of convenience and there's always a tradeoff. We don't want people to make extreme tradeoffs that inhibit their ability to do business or slow it down, but it should be felt a little bit. If people aren't complaining about information security a little bit, it means you're likely not doing your job. You want the presence of cybersecurity to be felt actively throughout the organization.

These secrets are tried-and-true methods that CISOs at organizations large and small have utilized to tremendous success. In an effort to standardize the way all organizations stay more secure, every security professional must become comfortable with the unknown and stay focused on keeping their tools, systems, and employees on their toes at all times. An organization's security is only as good as their CISO's leadership.

*As co-founder and chief operating officer at SecurityScorecard, **Sam Kassoumeh** is responsible for driving the company's product portfolio. With extensive experience as both a cybersecurity practitioner and leader, Sam's experience has been pivotal in the company's growth and development as well as in establishing the ecosystem risk management space. His passion for internet security started in his teens and propelled him into key cybersecurity roles including head of security and compliance at Gilt Groupe and worldwide InfoSec lead at Federal-Mogul. Sam holds a BBA in Management Information Systems from the University of Michigan-Dearborn.*

> **"**
>
> *No CISO is ever going to know everything about cybersecurity.*

12

C: The Cyber Landscape is Shifting: The CISO's Personality Matters

ADAM BISHOP, DIRECTOR,
INFORMATION SECURITY AT EPAM SYSTEMS

I was at a presentation once with a mixed security and non-security audience. The speaker asked, "Who here is in sales?" About 10 percent of the audience raised their hands.

The speaker then went on to give a security presentation, pointing out that the biggest part of being in security is selling your business-side colleagues on the importance of security measures, which are often things they don't want to do—for example, two-factor authentication, or security expenditures that can't directly return an investment. All of those are hard sells for your non-security colleagues, but if you work in security, and especially if you're a Chief Information Security Officer (CISO), you have to make these arguments every day. At the end of the presentation, the speaker asked again "Who here is in sales?" Everybody in the room raised their hand.

Being a good salesperson is just one of the traits CISOs need in order to successfully win the security battle.

I've held many jobs on my way to the CISO role. I went from answering phones to writing code to working with databases, which launched me into information security. Eventually, I was offered the opportunity to lead a company-wide effort to remediate power plants for something called NERC CIP, a federal regulation for utilities and generators to secure their power plants and infrastructure from cyber threat. That was my introduction to NIST, governance, and technical remediation. It led to a leadership role in security for a big energy company and eventually to my current role as the CEO of Cyber R&D Lab.

During my time at that organization, I remember more than anything what it was like working with my colleagues at the people level. The people you're working with define your organization, even more so than its capabilities. That's why every CISO's own personal traits and people skills are so vital to the success of their organization's security efforts.

The five necessary traits for CISOs

What are the most important personality traits for a CISO? CISOs vary, obviously, but certain soft skills set up a CISO—and by extension, an organization—for success more than some of the qualifications board members might see listed on a resume or a CV.

Willingness to learn

No CISO is ever going to know everything about security. Cybersecurity is a constantly changing field, so anyone who is in charge of security has to be willing to learn and can never become complacent. A CISO, or anybody in a leadership position with security, should understand that they'll never have the upper hand. The latest and greatest defenses are

already old news to the bad guys. A good CISO understands that the good guys learn more about security by watching what the bad guys do and adapt as quickly as possible to that new paradigm. They'll always be at least one step behind, and they have to be OK with that.

Being personally secure in their own vulnerabilities

A good CISO has to be able to sit across from the CEO and the board and be okay admitting that there are some risks they don't have a handle on yet. This can be difficult. As much as every CISO loves to say, "Well, we have these compensating measures and we have these risk mitigations," at the end of the day a good CISO knows those programs are not necessarily enough to prevent an organization from ending up in the headlines. That's what the board is really asking: "What is our risk? Can this breach happen to us?" It takes a certain kind of individual to honestly admit to the risks that exist and the gaps in time and resources that it takes to mitigate those risks. This level of emotional security is important. As a board, you want your CISO to listen to their team and give you the answers you need to hear not the answers they think you want to hear.

Flexibility

Because the technology field and security itself is always changing, the best CISOs are adaptable. They can adapt to new technologies, new threats, and new situations—like the fact that COVID-19 sent most of the workforce home. Any paradigm shift in the market—and there have been several—can be handled by an adaptable CISO. Take cloud computing: The cloud has completely changed the way CISOs think about security. The secure perimeter model is now obsolete. If your CISO is not adept at change and thinking differently about risk, your organization will have massive gaps and will be exploited, because you weren't flexible, and the attackers were.

There should be no sacred cows

Every organization has its sacred cows—particular practices or unwritten policies that might be built into company culture and go unchallenged by most employees including the C-suite. Take the example of a board member who is allowed to bring his personal, unsecure iPad into an organization that doesn't allow employees to bring tablets onto the premises. No tablets are allowed, but this iPad isn't questioned because it belongs to a board member. A good CISO doesn't blindly buy into any company culture that might prove risky from a security standpoint. Instead, they question everything even if it ruffles feathers at the highest levels.

The ability to embody more than one role

A CISO must be able to be a teacher, a salesperson, and a technologist all in one. That's not easy since these are often conflicting roles, and technology people and salespeople never agree. Engineers are not people people, yet a CISO has to be a person who can empathize with others and educate. CISOs have to be able to discuss everything from finance to perimeter control to cloud migration. The welfare and success of the company's security program rides on their ability to educate people at a high level—not just the board but the rest of the organization and the extended enterprise.

Why is it important for boards to know a CISO's traits?

Boards are tasked with choosing the CEO of a company and monitoring their performance. Companies are often described as a ship. The CEO's job is to run the company and steer the ship. The board's job is to make sure you have the right captain for that ship. Boards should do the same for the CISO, whose job is as critical to keeping the organization afloat as the CEO. If a CISO doesn't seem to have the personality traits described above, or if they tell board members everything they want to hear, that's often the sign of a problem.

Board members who aren't used to communicating with the CISO can get started by asking questions during presentations. They shouldn't limit themselves to expected questions, however. Instead, they should ask the questions the CISO hasn't prepped for. The worst thing a board can do is sit through 20 slides of infosec debrief and not ask a single question. It's the board's responsibility to create an environment where that debriefing can become a conversation.

The more technical board members should run point on this, but all board members should know the CISO.

Ensuring that the right person is in charge of security, and at every level of analysis, is key to the overall due diligence that the board is ultimately accountable for.

Adam Bishop has over 20 years of experience in information technology, information security, and risk management spanning a breadth of roles ranging from database administrator to CISO. Director, Information Security at EPAM Systems, Adam values a people-first and customer-first approach to innovative problem solving and risk mitigation.

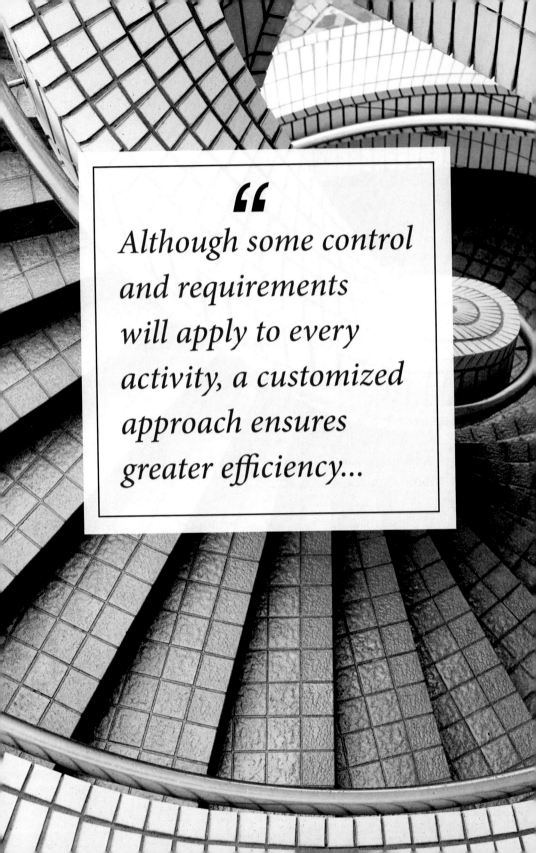

> **"**
> *Although some control
> and requirements
> will apply to every
> activity, a customized
> approach ensures
> greater efficiency...*

13

O: Operating in a Complex Regulatory Landscape

EDNA CONWAY, VP AND CHIEF SECURITY & RISK OFFICER, AZURE AT MICROSOFT

This chapter will dive into how security executives and their organizations can navigate and succeed in complex, globally-divergent regulatory landscapes.

The platform economy and its regulatory ramifications:

Security professionals can all agree: data is the lifeblood flowing through business operations in the digital age. At the same time, organizations have shifted to a platform economy, the foundation of which is built on cloud and mobility capabilities. While businesses have converged on that platform economy foundation, an increasingly complex regulatory landscape continues to grow across the globe. Navigating this landscape must be done in a manner that does not focus on mere compliance and, as a result, reduce fundamental security.

The complexity of this landscape is manifest in seven key areas showing commonality across new or expanding regulation, legislation, and standards:

1. Data privacy[1]
2. Digital identity
3. Identity provenance
4. Third-party and supply-chain risk management[2]
5. Platform and technology ethics
6. Export restrictions (encryption technology, ML/AI)[3]
7. Trade controls

Practitioners and users across the private and public sectors increasingly recognize that they need a holistic set of controls. As a result, particularly given the rise of the platform economy, mandated regulations and recommended standards now span:

- Technology development and fabrication, whether hardware or software
- Information technology configuration and operation
- Physical and functional scanning
- End of life/service management

As organizations increase their digital footprint, they need to meet compliance requirements across a complex, interconnected IT stack. Operating in the platform economy requires not only secure cloud resource configuration, but assessment of the core security practices of third-party cloud providers.

The controls and outcomes demanded by new or expanded regulations and standards extend from the basic to the highly specific. For example, a quick scan of U.S. National Institute of Standards & Technology (NIST) Special Publication 800-53 Revision 5 (September 2020) reveals that its 1,189 controls touch upon:

- Access control and enforcement (including account disablement, information-flow enforcement, separation of duties, least privilege, etc.)

- Authentication and encryption

- Mandatory content in audit records

- Information exchange (including transfer authorization and transitive exchange)

- Boundary protection

- Cryptographic mechanism implementation

- Sensor relocation

- Provenance establishment
- Data set de-identification
- Supply-chain risk management
- Component disposal

Meanwhile, less prescriptive mandates leave best practices open to interpretation. Security leaders looking to drive security across platforms struggle to balance these ever-expanding and geographically-divergent regulatory requirements.

A plan to address regulatory complexity

The answer to overcoming these challenges lies in a comprehensive security and resiliency architecture. As businesses increasingly rely on platforms, they need to take an architectural approach as they address the blending of risk, compliance, and security demands. However, it can't be just any architecture. It must be one that allows for mapping to regulatory requirements, as well as the international standards and certifications that address the concerns at the core of those regulations.

As a start, organizations can begin to weave regulatory directives into every level of operations overseen by security organizations. In doing so, they can constantly map and cross-map activities to international regulations and standards. These operations should include, at a minimum:

Risk and threat intelligence	• Keep abreast of developing security threats. • Help the company and board understand potential security problems that might arise.
Data-loss and fraud prevention	• Adhere to all laws and regulations. • Avoid the misuse or theft of data.
Security and resiliency architecture	• Holistically address government regulations, industry standards, trade and labor laws.
Identity and access management	• Ensure that only authorized people have access to resources. • Limit access to data essential to their respective roles.
Third-party engagement	• Know the "who, what and where" of the third-party ecosystem.
Investigations and forensics	• Gather and analyze evidence related to attempted attacks, breaches, and the threats of electronic or physical manipulation, espionage, or operational disruption together with mitigation planning.
Governance	• Continuously monitor the full spectrum of comprehensive security. • Policy oversight

Table 1

Fundamentally, all regulations and standards require compliance over these seven security categories, even when they diverge on how to implement the controls.

An Architectural Framework

To meet these compliance mandates while maintaining a robust cybersecurity posture, security leaders need to develop an architecture that allows for mapping to the regulatory requirements, international standards, and certifications that address core regulatory concerns.

Roadmap

While a roadmap acts as a first step, security professionals should establish a framework that provides empirical data to establish conformity with applicable regulations and internal standards across all operations' and solutions' lifecycles.

- Identify and analyze:
  - internal policies
  - external certifications schemes
  - international standards
  - cross-industry best practices
  - legal and regulatory mandates
- Develop a unified model with security and resiliency as the two pillars
- Establish fundamental domains under each pillar such as in Table 1
- Identify and establish sub-categories as in Table 2
- Develop controls and requirements for each domain and subdomain; create separate controls for internal and external members of your organization's ecosystem, and customize those controls and requirements based on the members to which they apply
- Prioritize control and requirement remediation based on risk:
  - Triage areas of non-compliance against the relevant regulatory standards

PILLAR	DOMAIN
Security	Security governance
Security	Personnel & behavioral management
Security	Asset management
Security	Physical security
Security	Manufacturing security
Security	Logistics security
Security	Security engineering & architecture
Security	Identity & access management
Security	Security operations
Security	Information protection
Security	Privacy
Security	Security incident management
Security	Supplier security
Resiliency	Resiliency governance
Resiliency	Business continuity/disaster recovery
Resiliency	Health & safety
Resiliency	Labor & human rights
Resiliency	Anti-bribery/anti-corruption
Resiliency	Trade & export control
Resiliency	Environmental sustainability

PILLAR	DOMAIN	SUBDOMAIN
Security	Security governance	Strategy and planning
Security	Security governance	Risk management
Security	Security governance	Reporting & Communication
Security	Security governance	Compliance & Accountability

Table 2

- o Evaluate penalties and remediation time frames
- o Consider the security impact and regulatory liability ramifications
- Develop a comprehensive map of all activities in which internal teams and third parties engage, with explanations or definitions of each activity

These steps allow security leaders to map controls and requirements to only those activities that are relevant. This process creates a uniform framework and avoids an inefficient monolithic approach, giving security executives the flexibility to focus on the unique aspects of a team's or third party's business. Although some control and requirements will apply to every activity, a customized approach ensures greater efficiency, efficacy, and compliance visibility.

A framework like this produces empirical data that both demonstrates integrity and serves as a map to comply with regulatory, legal, and industry standards mandates. Moreover, the security executive can swiftly revise the framework to assure compliance to new mandates, and adapt to new technologies, business models, and vulnerabilities.

From framework to ongoing engagement

After establishing the framework and its elements, ongoing engagement is imperative. The following 15 actions will assist in supporting security leaders as they tackle the vast and complex regulatory landscape, while also ensuring that they affirmatively engage internal and external stakeholders:

1. Create a close partnership with the legal department.

2. Engage and embrace ramifications of geopolitical and economic disruption.

3. Stay connected to engineering organizations including software, hardware, and services.

4. Communicate with executive management in business areas, such as finance or HR, to align priorities and interests and avoid conflicting policies.

5. Understand and stay abreast of the U.S. and international privacy law landscape.

6. Leverage a platform or service to facilitate regulatory compliance.

7. Work with the enterprise risk team to identify and properly prioritize the right risks.

8. Identify areas of potential impact, e.g. risks to continuity of supply of third-party-provided software, services, components, and raw materials.

9. Prioritize action plans by both likelihood of occurrence and severity of impact.

10. Establish criteria for addressing impacts.

11. Deploy a methodology for routine monitoring.

12. Develop a plan to mitigate risk impacts.

13. Consider the regulatory implications of sharing breach and vulnerability information.

14. Gain a seat at the table to influence corporate decisions.

15. Where possible, participate in public-private partnerships including government engagement.

Conclusion

Security leaders can overcome the significant challenges they face when operating in a complex regulatory landscape. With an architectural framework approach, they can maintain focus on their core mission—the security and resiliency of an organization's operations. A flexible architecture, like the framework described here, can adapt to meet any size organization's need to drive security and resiliency, while successfully navigating the complex global landscape.

Edna Conway *currently serves as VP and Chief Security & Risk Officer, Azure at Microsoft. She is responsible for the security, resiliency and governance of the cloud infrastructure upon which Microsoft's Intelligent Cloud business operates. She has built new organizations delivering trust, transparency, cybersecurity, compliance, risk management, sustainability and value chain transformation. Prior to joining Microsoft, Edna served as Cisco's Chief Security Officer, Global Value Chain, driving a comprehensive security architecture across Cisco's third-party ecosystem. She is recognized domestically (U.S. Presidential Commissions) and globally (NATO) as the developer of architectures delivering value chain security, sustainability and resiliency. Edna was appointed to the Executive Committee of the U.S. Department of Homeland Security Task Force on ICT Supply Chain Risk Management. Her insight is featured in a range of publications, analyst reports, and case studies, including Forbes, Fortune, Bloomberg, CIO Magazine and the Wall Street Journal. Recognition of her industry leadership includes membership in the Fortune Most Powerful Women community, and awards including: 2021 Top Cybersecurity Leaders (Security Magazine), Top 50 Women Leaders in SaaS (#5 – The Software Report 2020), Who's Who in Cybersecurity (Onalytica 2020), Fed 100 Award, Stevie Maverick of the Year Award, CSO of the Year Award at RSA,*

Machine to Machine and IOT Trailblazer Award (Connected World Magazine), Reboot Leadership Award (SC Media), Columbia University's Barnard College Distinguished Alumna Award 2019 and New Hampshire Tech Professional of the Year 2018 Award.

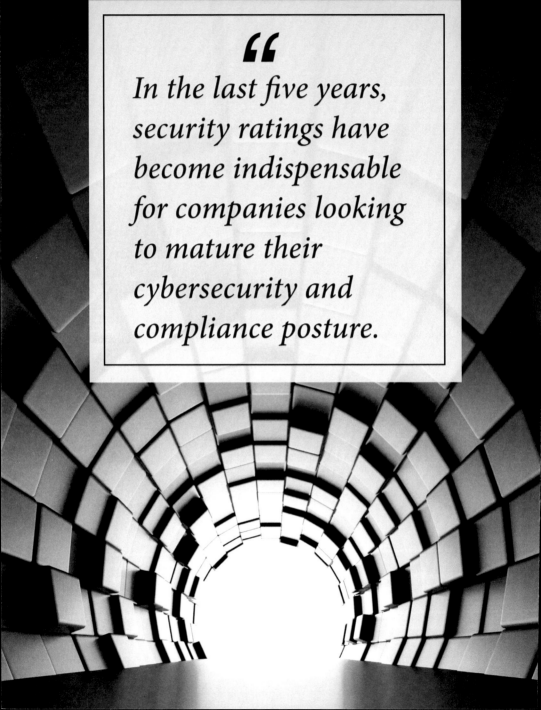

> **"** In the last five years, security ratings have become indispensable for companies looking to mature their cybersecurity and compliance posture.

14

R: Ratings Are the Future of Cybersecurity

ALEKSANDR YAMPOLSKIY, CEO AND CO-FOUNDER, SECURITYSCORECARD

Fifteen years ago, award-winning author Thomas Friedman wrote a prescient commentary on how technology was changing the way people worked:

> *The dynamic force in Globalization 3.0—the thing that gives it its unique character—is individuals and small groups globalizing. Individuals must, and can, now ask, "Where do I fit into the global competition and opportunities of the day, and how can I, on my own, collaborate with others globally?"*[1]

[1] Friedman, Thomas L. (2005). "It's a Flat World, After All." *The New York Times Magazine*. April 3, 2005. https://www.nytimes.com/2005/04/03/magazine/its-a-flat-world-after-all.html

Technology companies responded to Friedman's question about global collaboration by embracing digital transformation and placing mission-critical data and applications in the cloud. Organizations became more competitive by leveraging cloud-based resources to streamline operations and reduce costs, which also increased their digital footprints and cybersecurity risk.

Monitoring complex digital footprints

In November 2020, the World Economic Forum released *"Future Series: Cybersecurity, Emerging Technology, and Systemic Risk,"* a joint report with the University of Oxford.[2] The report detailed the ways in which systemic cybersecurity risks arising from the ubiquity of certain technologies and the interdependencies within supply chains can cripple a global economy, stating, "The emergence of new products and growth of new service-based models is creating complex interdependencies between organisations, supply chains, sectors and individuals." Equally important, the World Economic Forum recommends utilizing integrated cybersecurity tools to support intelligence sharing and keep pace with a dynamic threat landscape.

In the last five years, security ratings have become indispensable for companies looking to mature their cybersecurity and compliance posture. Security ratings platforms scan an organization's digital footprint, detecting control weaknesses, alerting security teams to vulnerabilities, and suggesting risk mitigation activities. They can also be used to passively scan third-party ecosystems, helping companies gain a comprehensive view of risk within their vendor ecosystem. Ratings platforms then assign a score based on how well a company is performing across different cyber risk factors. A higher score indicates a more robust security program, while a lower score indicates vulnerabilities need to be remediated.

---

[2] World Economic Forum. (2020). "Future Series: Cybersecurity, emerging technology, and systemic risk." *World Economic Forum.* November 2020. http://www3.weforum.org/docs/WEF_Future_Series_Cybersecurity_emerging_technology_and_systemic_risk_2020.pdf

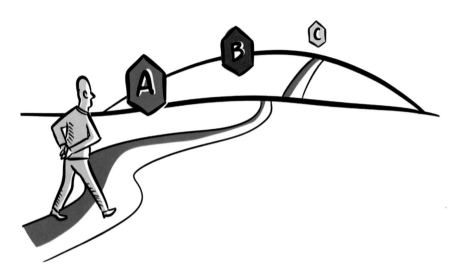

As organizations look to further expand their cloud deployments, security ratings provide valuable insights that enable stronger partnerships between organizations working to create a more secure business ecosystem.

Bridging the Language Gap

As companies undergo digital transformation, the same technologies that support growth also drive cybersecurity risk, which threatens business continuity. This highlights the need for security leaders to communicate about cyber risk in business terms so executives and board members can make informed decisions around vendor onboarding and technology adoption—for example, explaining that spending $200,000 on a solution that reduces the likelihood of a denial of service attack can help avoid a $3 million loss for the business.

Security ratings platforms also bridge the gap in security expertise by distilling granular data into more easily understood high-level categories that communicate business risk. Technical data and controls, such as open access points and insecure or misconfigured

SLL certificates, are rated in a business-level risk category like "network security" so business leaders can obtain a broad view of cyber risk.

Establishing Accountability

In recent years, regulatory agencies have increasingly looked to hold business leaders accountable for corporate privacy and security. The Federal Trade Commission imposed a $5 billion penalty on one CEO for their company's user privacy decisions in 2019.[3] Meanwhile, the California Consumer Privacy Act (CCPA), now incorporated into the California Privacy Rights Act (CPRA), allows consumers to pursue civil action to recover damages, obtain injunctive or declaratory relief, or obtain any other relief the court deems proper.[4] These changes indicate a broad shift toward holding organizations and their governing bodies responsible for their data security and privacy policies. To meet their fiduciary duty to their investors and shareholders, executives and boards need to understand how data privacy and risk intersect with their operational objectives.

According to IBM's *"Cost of a Data Breach Report 2020,"* 46% of respondents said that the CISO is most responsible for the occurence of a data breach.[5] The same report also found that only 27% of respondents said the CISO plays a significant role in shaping cybersecurity policy and technology decision-making. These data points indicate a broken line of accountability, shown by the disparity between the CISO's level of input and the blame they ultimately carry when an adverse event occurs.

[3] Federal Trade Commission. (2019). "FTC Imposes $5 Billion Penalty and Sweeping New Privacy Restrictions on Facebook." *Federal Trade Commission*. July 24, 2019. https://www.ftc.gov/news-events/press-releases/2019/07/ftc-imposes-5-billion-penalty-sweeping-new-privacy-restrictions

[4] California Privacy Rights Act. 2020. https://www.oag.ca.gov/system/files/initiatives/pdfs/19-0021A1%20%28Consumer%20Privacy%20-%20Version%203%29_1.pdf

[5] IBM Security. (2020). "Cost of a Data Breach Report 2020." IBM Security. 2020. https://www.ibm.com/security/data-breach

Under the appropriate reporting structure, CISOs are able to play a more significant role in shaping the policies that lead to the outcomes they are held responsible for. With the right tools, they can translate their technical expertise into important operational insights for the business. Security ratings provide the shared language necessary to drive those conversations, and the monitoring capabilities to be proactive in their day-to-day security operations. In fact, it has been found that companies with security ratings scores of 'F' are 7.7x more likely to experience a breach than companies with an 'A.'[6] Forward-thinking leadership teams embrace security ratings as a path to better business practices, and ultimately a safer world.

Driving resilience in the digital supply chain

Security ratings also offer critical insights into supply-chain risk and allow security teams to be proactive rather than reactive. Cyber resilience can be visualized as three concentric circles. The first layer consists of data stored on premises, typically protected by traditional controls like firewalls. The second layer consists of the organization's users and devices that connect to the internet. Finally, the third layer consists of the third-party ecosystem. This last layer, the supply chain, is the greatest risk most companies face, because they often lack visibility into and control over this extensive ecosystem.

Just as security ratings create a common language for discussing cyber risk internally, they can also be used to create a base level of trust within the supply chain. A cyber-resilient organization invests more heavily in these solutions which enable transparency and collaboration between business partners. When organizations align service level contractual agreements to objective cybersecurity metrics, they can establish and enforce a set of shared security principles and expectations.

[6] Aminian, Negin. (2020). "Optimizing SecurityScorecard Ratings with Machine Learning." *SecurityScorecard*. December 1, 2020. https://securityscorecard.com/blog/optimizing-securityscorecard-ratings-with-machine-learning

Security ratings offer CISOs and corporate leadership the visibility to track risk and remediation within the supply chain and a basis for fact-based conversations about security issues.

Security ratings are here to stay

Much like credit ratings, security ratings appear to be here to stay. Regulators use their continuous monitoring capabilities as ongoing assurance of an organization's compliance posture. Customers look to them when choosing software services and applications. Within industries, organizations will compare their security ratings with those of their peers much as they engage in annual financial analyses.

According to Forrester, "Cybersecurity ratings are just emerging as tools for talking about cybersecurity risk with the board, having historically been the province of security professionals. Forrester expects cybersecurity ratings to become a de facto standard in the boardroom by 2025. Investors and traditional debt ratings agencies will include cybersecurity as a risk factor for rating the ability to repay company debt (influenced in part by the cybersecurity ratings market). As cybersecurity becomes part of debt financing discussions, directors will expect security leaders to show how their cybersecurity program can help drive down these costs. Security leaders will review cybersecurity ratings during regular board discussions and should expect their cybersecurity program to make ratings improvement part of regular business-as-usual activities."

Forrester's reporting suggests that cyber risk ratings will play an important role in assessing a company's overall financial viability. This portends well for an increasingly connected business ecosystem, in which malicious actors more often than not infiltrate an organization's network via a third party. Widespread collaboration, intelligence sharing, and adoption of security ratings represent the clearest path to making business ecosystems, and the world, safer for everyone.

Aleksandr Yampolskiy is a globally recognized cybersecurity innovator, leader, and expert. As co-founder and chief executive officer, Alex has led the company since its beginnings in 2013 to become one of the world's most trusted cybersecurity brands. His vision is to create a new language for cybersecurity by enabling people to work collaboratively across the enterprise and with external parties to build a more secure ecosystem. Prior to founding the company, Alex was a hands-on CTO at Cinchcast and BlogTalkRadio, the largest online talk radio and podcast hosting platform. Prior to that, he led security and compliance at Gilt Groupe, where he managed all aspects of IT infrastructure security, secure application development, and PCI compliance. Alex has a B.A. in mathematics and computer science from New York University and a Ph.D. in Cryptography from Yale University.

> **"**
> *In the next 10 years, more CISOs must evolve their mindset from managing risks to helping their businesses win through operational resilience.*

15

E: The Evolving Role of the CISO

CHARLES BLAUNER, PARTNER AND CISO IN RESIDENCE, TEAM8 VENTURES

In the beginning, the mission given to the Chief Information Security Officer (CISO) by their organization was simple: "Keep us out of trouble."

Back in the late 1990s, when I took my first CISO job at JP Morgan, the role was all about keeping the bad guys out and ensuring the organization was compliant with regulations. In the 20 years since, the CISO job has evolved and become more nuanced. By the time I retired from my last job at Citigroup, all my conversations with business leaders were about managing risk.

Now a new breed of CISO is emerging. CISOs are evolving from simply managing infosec and cyber risk to becoming more concerned about the operational resilience of their organizations, and becoming business enablers. It is the next step in an evolutionary process that started with the CISO being the executive who might have appeared before the board once a year, because the law required it, and is now seeing the CISO become a fully-realized member of the senior management team.

A brief history of the CISO

While information security has been around for a long time, there were no CISOs or information security programs in the 1980s. At that time, IT and security departments were responsible for information security, and that work was mostly limited to managing access to corporate mainframes. With the advent of dial-up modems, however, corporate networks started to be exposed to the outside world, and hackers started to find those networks. In response, a broader security function started to emerge in many corporations, although it was still in the domain of the IT department.

Then in 1994, Citibank was hacked, losing $10 million to Russian hacker Vladimir Levin. In response, Citibank created a senior executive position tasked with owning information security, hiring Steve Katz as the first-ever CISO in 1995. Slowly but surely, other banks and large enterprises started to follow suit.

For years, the CISO was seen as a technology role. The CISO's job was to keep companies in compliance and out of trouble. And, even though the CISO was technically a member of the C-suite, most CEOs had no idea who the CISO was. Nor did the board, who in banks, only saw the CISO once a year because the Gramm-Leach-Bliley Act required it. Most non-banking CISOs never even met the board of directors.

That's not the case today. Over the last 20 years, the role of the CISO has shifted to one of risk management. Nowadays, most CISOs get regular face time with their CEO and boards of directors. The C-suite

knows their name. But that's not enough. In the long run, the thing most CISOs want is for the CEO and the senior leadership team to come to the CISO and say, "Come sit with us and be a part of the business discussion."

What's holding CISOs back from a senior business role?

One of the challenges facing CISOs is definitional. They're seen as being in charge of cybersecurity when their job is information security—and these two things are not the same. When there's a data breach, it is most often the CISO who is held responsible, irrespective of actual responsibility.

The fact of the matter is that most CISOs are not responsible for all aspects of cybersecurity. In most organizations, there's a shared responsibility for cyber among the CISO, CTO, and CIO. Boards often don't understand this shared responsibility, and when there's a data breach, they do the easy, obvious thing: fire the CISO. It is critical for management to clearly articulate responsibility and accountability for all aspects of cyber to the board of directors.

A second challenge is that many CISOs hold themselves back by sticking to operational metrics when they report to their boards. This is an approach that actually holds their boards back when it comes to understanding what CISOs really do, and it plays into the fact that most boards get slightly nervous when the CISO appears in a meeting. They see the CISO as a technical expert who may, at best, present information that they don't completely understand and, at worst, inform them of a problem.

When a CISO talks about metrics, they're treating their board like a management group instead of a board. When they frame that report in the context of risk tolerance, however, they take the first step towards changing their board's perception of the CISO role. It's a much more engaging conversation and is exactly the sort of discussion a board should be having with a senior executive.

This isn't always easy for technically-minded CISOs. Some find it challenging to translate technical risk into a business context, but it's important. Once a CISO is talking about organizational business risk rather than technical risks, their colleagues on the business side will be much more likely to pay attention.

Where is the CISO role headed?

The long-term mission of any business is to win—to grow, expand, and be profitable. The new breed of CISO shares these goals. In the next 10 years, more CISOs must evolve their mindset from managing risks to helping their businesses win through operational resilience.

In order to take on that evolved role, the first necessary step is a change in duties. CISOs must truly start managing cyber risk for their firm, becoming responsible for continuity of business, and more broadly, technology risk management. If they are not already, the CISO should be a peer of the CIO with direct access to the CEO and unfiltered access to the board of directors.

While CISOs will continue to think of all the same challenges their predecessors have thought about historically, namely risks and threats, they'll now frame those challenges from the perspective of their organizations' mission and critical processes. This means really understanding what an organization's critical business processes are, and what the specific risks to them are.

The CISO of the future's focus will have to become less about technology and more about the business, so the skills the CISO will need will vary based to some degree on the industry they are in. CISOs at banks need to understand the business of banking. A CISO at a consumer goods company must know as much about manufacturing and physical supply chains as the other C-level executives in the organization. That knowledge will help them protect their firms' most valuable assets and increase the company's profitability.

Just because the CISO will have to frame everything in a business context does not mean the new breed of CISO will be coming from the business side of an organization. Future CISOs are out there right now working in the security teams we are building, but to help them become more business-focused, we have to do a good job at staff development.

Future CISOs may currently be in roles like CIO or Head of Operations —any role that focuses on risk and operational resiliency. Some companies, JP Morgan for example, are doing this right now. The CISO at JP Morgan is responsible for tech risk and is also considered a CIO.

And it goes both ways—both of the last two CISOs at JP Morgan are still with the firm in business-line CIO roles.

The natural side effect of the CISO taking a business-oriented role will be noticeable. In the past, the CEO might not have known their name, but now the CEO is going to seek out the CISO. Why? The CISO is no longer talking about a technical subject. Now they're talking about how they're going to help the business make more money and become more resilient.

Charles Blauner is an internationally recognized expert independent advisor on Cyber Resiliency, Information Security Risk Management and Data Privacy. Charles is a Partner and CISO in Residence at Team8 Ventures and a Venture Advisor at the Cyber Mentors Fund. Charles is also the President of Cyber Aegis, a boutique cyber risk management consultancy. Previously, Charles had a distinguished career working on Information Security for over 30 years, with 25 years being in Financial Services including being the Chief Information Security Officer (CISO) at JP Morgan and Deutsche Bank, and most recently the Global Head of Information Security at Citi. During this time, Charles held numerous industry leadership roles including Chair of the Financial Services Sector Coordinating Council (FSSCC), founding Director of the Financial Services Information Sharing and Analysis Center (FS-ISAC), and the Chair of the OpenGroup's Security Program. Charles has worked closely with banking regulators around the world including the OCC, FRB, BoE, MAS, and HKMA to help reduce the risk posed by cyber threats to the financial sector at large. Charles is a regular conference speaker and has had the honor of appearing in front of US House and Senate committees. In 2015, Charles was recognized by his peers, winning the Wasserman Award, which recognizes outstanding career achievement and contribution to the Information Systems Audit, Control, Security, Risk Management, and/or Governance professions. Charles has a M.S. in Computer Science from the University of Southern California (USC) and a B.S. in Computer Science from Rensselaer Polytechnic Institute (RPI).

"

Building trust is the foundation of an empathetic relationship between the CISO and the board of directors.

16

Conclusion: Why Trust is Critical to a CISO's Success

DR. TAHER ELGAMAL, CTO OF SECURITY, SALESFORCE

"It is not just the possibility of contagion between companies and nations that creates systemic risk, but the world's mutual reliance on shared, critical global services which underpin global trade, finance, security and transport."[1] —Klaus Schwab

In his book, *Shaping the Fourth Industrial Revolution*, author Klaus Schwab details how truly disruptive emerging technologies bring promises of a brighter future and new risks that can undermine global

---

[1] Schwab, K. (2018). *Shaping the future of the fourth industrial revolution: A guide to building a better world.* New York: Currency. pp.114-115.

economies. Citing a Carnegie Mellon University survey statistic, Schwab notes that 77% of US board members rarely or never received senior leadership reports regarding digital privacy or security risks as recently as 2008.[2] However, twelve years later, cyber risk has emerged as a fundamental business concern equal to financial risk and certainly harder to quantify. Despite the impact cyber risk has on organizational stability, security professionals still struggle to measure, manage, and mitigate it because research is still in its nascent state. To fully address cyber risk's impact on market conditions, boards and CISOs need to build trust by working collectively both within their organizations and across their peer groups.

Building trust and empathy

Building trust is the foundation of an empathetic relationship between the CISO and the board of directors. Business leaders often forget, particularly in the technology space, that empathy strengthens an organization. By working together, directors and CISOs can use trust and empathy to enhance their cybersecurity posture.

Creating a common language acts as an entry point. As the individuals responsible for executing technical programs, CISOs understand details around an attack like the vulnerability exploited or the CVE number. Successful CISOs also need business risk knowledge, or a willingness to learn it, to communicate these technical risks in the way that directors can relate to.

However, every dance requires two people. Although many articles claim that CISOs must speak the language of business, few note that board members need to learn the fundamentals of cybersecurity. Directors need to prove their commitment to finding a common language so that they can engage in dialogue. When the CISO explains

---

[2] Schwab, 111.

a risk to an asset, the board needs to respond with how they will gain the knowledge necessary to enable their CISO.

Building this trust and empathy starts with the board and CEO because, in the end, people follow their boss's lead. When their boards and CEOs recognize cyber risk's importance to the organization, security teams feel trusted leading to a symbiotic, empathetic relationship based on mutual trust and respect. The CISO knows the board needs to understand how cyber risk impacts the business's bottom line, while the board recognizes that the CISO needs the tools to manage the technical aspects of the program. By building a trusting and empathetic relationship, they can work together to recover from a data security incident knowing that both sides did their due diligence.

Boards need to view their CISOs as both business partners and technology experts. CISOs need to respond in kind by learning how their organization views business risk in the context of technology. By working together and learning from one another, boards and CISOs establish a common risk language that enables them to establish a trusting, empathetic relationship.

Quantifying risk

Common language matters because boards exist to protect their organizations from risk. Most directors are business or financial experts because traditional corporate risks are focused on those areas. For example, while board members need to sign attestations that they know how to read and interpret financial reports, no equivalent cybersecurity requirement exists. Historically, this makes sense because researchers have established sophisticated financial risk models over the last century or more. By contrast, cybersecurity risks have existed for a mere 25 years, and they continue to evolve making management and mitigation difficult. During the early days of e-commerce, fraud risks were the most important, which increased with electronic banking. As enterprise infrastructures became more sophisticated, cybercriminals developed more sophisticated attacks. Ransomware, for example, could never have been foreseen in those early ecommerce years, and yet, it is one of the most prevalent threats today.

Boards and CISOs need to work together to quantify cybersecurity risk. Over the years, financial risk metrics evolved. For example, the FBI reports on the average cost of a data breach, and data has a monetary value on the dark web, which gives companies a way to quantify how a data breach impacts financial risk. In contrast, reputational risk remains more elusive. Traditional reputational risks all rely on internal actors with malicious intent—such as executives who make side deals with customers, or individuals embezzling money or selling stocks based on insider information. When these events occur, they show poor oversight and failed business processes.

Data breaches, however, often occur despite a security team's best efforts. A single mistake within the organization's IT infrastructure or across the supply chain can lead to a data breach. One device lacking an antivirus update or one successful phishing attack can lead to disastrous repercussions, but a single control failure does not necessarily indicate poor business processes and oversight. Engaging in due diligence mitigates reputational risk by proving commitment to protecting the organization, but it still cannot prevent a data breach. Organizations cannot easily quantify the financial impact of a damaged reputation after a data breach.

Working toward creating a collective defense strategy

In the geopolitical realm, collective defense means that an attack on one ally equates to an attack against the group of allied nations.[3] In cybersecurity, collective defense means having a direct exchange of experience and information. Cybercriminals will likely use successful attack methodologies against multiple companies within an industry. Unfortunately, a company's leadership often relies solely on analyst insights around cyberattack trends. Although valuable, these only provide an outsider's view. Organizations need to discuss together how attacks flow across an organization's infrastructure and what the attack's impact was. For example, analysts offer valuable insight into rising ransomware trends, which creates awareness. Ideally, a collective defense strategy can provide insight into the vulnerability exploited or the software version on a virtual machine that cybercriminals used.

On an informal level, CISOs have begun to create these types of communities. They meet regularly either within a geographic region or industry vertical to connect, often sharing the technical aspects of their experiences. These CISOs then bring this information back to their organizations or boards and provide insight into emerging risks. This

---

[3] 2019. "Collective defence – Article 5." *NATO*. November 25, 2019. https://www.nato.int/cps/en/natohq/topics_110496.htm

knowledge sharing is the cybersecurity version of collective defense. However, this all needs to happen in "web speed" to be effective.

Board members need to move towards a similar collective defense model within their peer community. For example, the National Association of Corporate Directors (NACD) incorporated a Cybersecurity Leadership Symposium for the first time at its 2020 convention.[4] The Symposium provided practical tips during the three-hour expert-led session including the importance of oversight, the impact of creating a cyber-risk oversight committee and the types of metrics to review. This symposium is an essential first step for directors, but they need to apply this knowledge to their own experiences. They need to work toward a collective defense strategy at the board level and use that to set the tone for their cybersecurity program.

These conversations need to start happening either formally or informally, because no organization exists in a vacuum. In the same way that directors discuss the global economy's financial impact on their organizations, they need to discuss the financial impact cybersecurity has on their organizations. They need to come together and listen to each others' experiences such as financial losses from cyber breaches, impressions of partners, and reasons for choosing one technology vendor over another. By sharing these experiences within their peer group, board members can more effectively work with their CISOs to be the resources their CISOs need.

Connectivity to collaborate for collective defense

For collective defense, cybersecurity strategies to be effective, and CISOs and directors need to connect with others who share the same goals to collaborate. Malicious actors are successful partially because they use connectivity to their advantage such as sharing

---

4 2020. "Cybersecurity Leadership Symposium Agenda." *NACD.* 2020. http://nacd.cms-plus.com/files/Cybersecurity_Leadership_Symposium.pdf

successful exploits in forums. Board members need to start thinking like cybercriminals and use the same connectivity principles. Too often, directors silo their knowledge worried that a competitor will take their market share. However, this competitive mentality leaves them and their businesses at risk. For example, energy sector organizations are just beginning to work together and are already seeing a return on that intellectual capital investment. Meanwhile the financial services sector CISOs have been cooperating for years. As CISOs and directors work together more closely within their organizations, they also need to reach out to peers with similar security goals.

A collective defense strategy requires that everyone work together toward a common goal. Countries need to set aside their differences and work together for the collective defense of information. In the same way that governments form alliances during physical wars, they need to establish partnerships for cyber wars. More minds are always more effective because diversity leads to innovation. The only way to protect an organization's financial stability is to work together to protect global economic stability. This means establishing a collective cyber-defense strategy across for-profit, non-profit, public, and private entities.

Dr. Taher Elgamal is the Chief Technology Officer for Security at Salesforce, and is an internationally respected information security leader and cryptographer. Dr. Elgamal was awarded the Marconi Prize for development of SSL/TLS recognizing his achievements and advancements made in the field of communications. He was the recipient of the lifetime achievement award from the RSA Conference in 2009. He has successfully served as CISO, Chief Scientist, CTO as well as Founder and CEO of numerous key organizations. Dr. Elgamal invented several industry and government standards in data security and digital signatures for areas including the DSS government standard for digital signatures. He is recognized in the industry as the "father of SSL".

About the Author

Aleksandr Yampolskiy is a globally recognized cybersecurity innovator, leader, and expert. As co-founder and chief executive officer, Alex has led the company since its beginnings in 2013 to become one of the world's most trusted cybersecurity brands. His vision is to create a new language for cybersecurity by enabling people to work collaboratively across the enterprise and with external parties to build a more secure ecosystem. Prior to founding the company, Alex was a hands-on CTO at Cinchcast and BlogTalkRadio, the largest online talk radio and podcast hosting platform. Prior to that, he led security and compliance at Gilt Groupe, where he managed all aspects of IT infrastructure security, secure application development, and PCI compliance. Alex has a B.A. in mathematics and computer science from New York University and a Ph.D. in Cryptography from Yale University.

About SecurityScorecard

SecurityScorecard is the global leader in cybersecurity ratings with millions of companies continuously rated. SecurityScorecard Ratings offer easy-to-read 'A-F' ratings across ten groups of risk factors including DNS health, IP reputation, web application security, network security, leaked information, hacker chatter, endpoint security, and patching cadence. SecurityScorecard Ratings evaluate an organization's cybersecurity risk using data-driven, objective, and continuously evolving metrics that provide visibility into any organization's information security control weaknesses as well as potential vulnerabilities throughout the supply chain ecosystem.

Founded in 2013 by security and risk experts Dr. Aleksandr Yampolskiy and Sam Kassoumeh, SecurityScorecard's patented rating technology is used by thousands of organizations for enterprise risk management, third-party risk management, board reporting, due diligence, and cyber insurance underwriting. SecurityScorecard continues to make the world a safer place by transforming the way companies understand, improve and communicate cybersecurity risk to their boards, employees and vendors. Every company has the universal right to their trusted and transparent Instant SecurityScorecard Rating.